ADVANCED WORD PROCESSING APPLICATIONS

JOB-BASED TASKS

Lloyd D. Brooks

Management Information Systems
Memphis State University
Memphis, Tennessee

Editor	Sonja Brown
Copy Editor	Laura Beaudoin
Text Design	Mori Studio
Cover Design	Joan Silver

ACKNOWLEDGEMENTS

Special thanks to the instructors and technical experts who contributed to this workbook:

Edward J. Coburn, Consultant
Rapid City, South Dakota

Peg Shroyer, Instructor
Itasca Community College
Grand Rapids, Minnesota

Julie A. Fasciana, Consultant
St. Paul, Minnesota

WordPerfect is a registered trademark of WordPerfect Corporation.
Microsoft Word is a registered trademark of Microsoft Corporation.
Lotus and 1-2-3 are registered trademarks of Lotus Development
     Corporation.
dBASE is a registered trademark of Ashton-Tate Publishing Group.

Library of Congress Cataloging-in-Publication Data

Brooks, Lloyd D., 1942-
     Advanced word processing applications: job-based tasks / Lloyd D.
Brooks.
          p.   cm.
     ISBN 1-56118-382-2
     1. Word processing.   I. Title.
HF5548.115.B748   1992
652.5—dc20   91-37551
                                                              CIP

Printed in the United States of America.

10 9 8 7 6 5 4 3 2 1

Contents

To the Student

The development of the microcomputer and accompanying software has changed the way that written communications are produced in business environments. Knowing how to use a word processing program to complete a variety of documents will be very useful in your career as well as in your personal life.

Initially, word processing was performed almost entirely by office support personnel. Ease of use and the availability of microcomputers and word processing software have made it essential for management level personnel to know word processing skills also. While this text is directed primarily toward helping prepare office personnel for the automated office, persons preparing for a wide multitude of business careers can benefit from the program.

Applications are organized into four units, with a scenario at the end of each unit to integrate and reinforce the skills presented in the unit. Itemized instructions and review questions will help you complete each application in a logical manner. If you use the Word-Perfect program, you will especially appreciate the tutorial at the end of the text.

Basic functions are mixed with advanced functions to provide you with a comprehensive instructional program. Best wishes for an enjoyable and worthwhile learning experience as you use the microcomputer to complete the practical, realistic applications.

Lloyd D. Brooks

Introduction

This book provides a series of word processing applications for you to complete. You can use any brand of equipment or commercial software program.

The applications are grouped into four major job performances: (1) using basic line and page formatting techniques in a variety of business correspondence; (2) practicing page formatting techniques in a variety of business correspondence and reports; (3) practicing document formatting techniques in a variety of business correspondence and in complex reports and manuscripts; and (4) manipulating and creating master documents with advanced word processing functions. Within each category, the difficulty of applications varies. The degree of thought and the complexity of functions determine the difficulty level.

General Instructions

Each application is presented on an assignment sheet. If specific instructions on the assignment sheets differ from the general instructions given here, follow the specific instructions on the assignment sheets. The following guidelines cover most of the procedures you will need to complete the applications.

1. After completing an application, submit the assignment sheet from this book together with a copy of the printed material requested in the application to your instructor for evaluation. Many of the assignment sheets contain questions relating to some aspect of the application. Answer these questions in the space provided on the assignment sheet prior to submitting the sheet and printed material to your instructor.

2. Use a 6.5-inch line from the left to the right margin for all applications, except where a different line length is indicated on the assignment sheet.

3. Some applications involve using material completed in a previous application. In these instances, you can retrieve the previously completed document from your data disk or from the Paradigm data disk (in the event you did not complete the previous application).

4. Files on the Paradigm data disk are stored in two formats: WordPerfect®, version 5.0, and ASCII. The WordPerfect files can be used with version 5.0 and later versions. The ASCII format can be retrieved into a variety of word processing programs.

   If you retrieve files in the ASCII format, you may lose some basic formatting features such as underlining and boldfacing. However, the basic text will be retrieved, and you can add the lost formatting features with your program.

5. Each application begins with a list of steps to complete the document. These steps also help you organize your approach to preparing the final printed piece. Material needed for the application is also provided. Most applications include Hints and Review questions that help you follow the recommended techniques or procedures.

6. Command cards are included in the back of this book for persons using WordPerfect and Microsoft Word®. These command cards contain basic commands for functions needed to complete the applications. If you are using a software program other than those listed, you may need to check your software manual to review the basic commands.

Proofreaders' Marks

The rough draft changes you will need to make in many applications are indicated with standard proofreaders' marks. An explanation of these symbols appears on pages 141-142.

Unit 1

Line Formatting

The first three applications in this unit present a quick review of fundamental word processing functions. You will review text editing features within the context of business letters and memorandums.

In Application 4 you will develop a customer list, a document that is used in a variety of businesses. In Application 5 you will prepare a simple newsletter, creating the look of columns by using wide margins.

Applications 6 and 7 include practice in reformatting text within letters and drawing lines to create an invoice form. You will revise stored documents in Applications 8, 9, and 10. Application 11 presents a simulated work problem that requires using the features and functions covered in this unit.

Application 1 **Letter**

---

1. Key the letter shown in Example A, using the default format of your word processing program. If you are using the Paradigm data disk, retrieve the ASCII file AEXER1 or the WordPerfect file PEXER1. Note: Some of the coding will be lost as revisions are made. If so, add the coding (such as paragraph indentions, underlining, and variable spacing) to the document.

2. Notice that the word "complete" is used three times in the second paragraph. Change the second use to a word with the same meaning so that the word will not appear twice in the same sentence.

3. In the first sentence boldface "Time Management Seminar." Boldface the word "faster" in the second sentence of paragraph 2. Also boldface the words "save time" in the first sentence of paragraph 3.

4. Save the revised document as EXER1.

5. Print one copy of the letter.

6. Your boss has marked some editing changes on the letter you have prepared. Retrieve the file EXER1.

7. Make the revisions indicated in Example B. Then print a copy of the revised letter.

8. Save the revised document as EXER1.

Complete the entire exercise before answering the review questions.

Review

1. On what line does the current date appear?_____

   _____

2. What keystroke sequence is used to boldface text? _____

   _____

3. What is the appropriate spacing following the writer's name
   for the reference initials and enclosure notation?

   _____

4. Why was the enclosure notation added to the letter?

   _____

   _____

5. If your software does not reformat automatically (adjust
   lines) after revisions, did you remember to reformat the text
   after revisions were made? _____

6. Did you replace the original file EXER1 with the revised
   document? _____

Example A

Current Date

Mr. John R. Billings
913 Coleman Avenue
Atlanta, GA 30354

Dear Mr. Billings:

Thank you for inquiring about the Time Management Seminar
that will be located in your city in a few months.

The seminar will provide many hints that will be helpful as
you complete your work and improve efficiency while you
complete office tasks. You will find ways to work faster
and complete more activities in a short period of time.
This will permit you to work in an environment where time is
used in the most efficient way possible.

This eight-hour seminar will help you save time which can
help you and others to increase productivity in your Georgia
office. A brochure is enclosed to provide additional information about the seminar.

Sincerely yours,

(Miss) Sarah W. Craig, Director
Professional Development Programs

ri

Enclosure

Current Date

Mr. John R. Billings
913 Coleman Avenue
Atlanta, GA 30354

Dear Mr. Billings:

Thank you for inquiring about the **Time Management Seminar** that will be located in your city in a few ~~months.~~ weeks

The seminar will provide many ~~hints~~ ideas that will be helpful as you complete your work and improve efficiency while you perform office tasks. You will find ways to work **faster** and complete more activities in a short~~er~~ period of time. This will permit you to work in an environment where time is used ~~in the most~~ efficient~~ly~~ ~~way possible.~~

This ~~eight~~ six-hour seminar will help ~~you~~ **save time** ~~which~~ to ~~can~~ help you and others ~~to~~ increase productivity in your ~~Georgia~~ Atlanta office. ~~A~~ The ~~brochure is~~ enclosed ~~to~~ provide~~s~~ additional information about the seminar.

Sincerely,

~~(Miss)~~ Sarah W. Craig, Director
Professional Development Programs

ri

Enclosure

Application 2 Memorandum

1. Key the memorandum in Example A, using the default format of your word processing program.

<table>
<tr><td>

Hint
_____

Did you use "Caps Lock" to key the memo title at the top?

</td></tr>
</table>

2. Underline the words "anticipated" and "next" in paragraph 1. Boldface the word "outstanding" in the last sentence of the memo.

3. Compute the number of keystrokes required during a 30-minute timing if 250 keystrokes are required per minute. Add this value to the sentence in the second paragraph to indicate the keystrokes required for 30 minutes. What is this value?

   _____

<table>
<tr><td>

Hint
_____

Set a tab 10 spaces from the left margin to key the To, From, Date, and Subject entries.

</td></tr>
</table>

4. Check the memo for language that might violate affirmative action guidelines. If such language is present, delete the sentence containing the language. What is the sentence?

   _____

5. Save the file as EXER2.

6. Print a copy of the memo.

7. Your boss has edited the memo you prepared. Retrieve the file EXER2 and make the changes shown in Example B.

8. Print a copy of the revised memo.

9. Save the revised document as EXER2.

> Complete the entire exercise before answering the review questions.

Review

1. What keystroke sequence did you use to center the title?

   _____

2. What equation did you use to compute the number of keystrokes for the 30-minute period? _____

   _____

3. If your software provides a sentence deletion feature, did you use that feature in instances where sentences were deleted?

   _____

   What was the keystroke sequence?_____

4. Why do you think the statement you chose to delete violates affirmative action guidelines? _____

   _____

   _____

   _____

5. What keystroke sequence did you use to underline text?

   _____

Example A

M E M O R A N D U M

TO: Ada Jane Walters, Director
           Personnel Services

FROM: Bret R. Canty, Manager
           Office Support Services

DATE: Current Date

SUBJECT: Employment Needs

There is an anticipated opening in the office support
services area for next month.

A vacancy resulted after one of our employees, Robert
Fults, was promoted to the Microcomputer Technical Resources Department to fill an opening in that area.
Robert has been in our department for almost two years.
Prospective candidates for the position should be able to
keyboard a minimum of 250 keystrokes per minute or
keystrokes during a 30-minute timing. A minimum of two
years of college is required as an educational requirement. The candidate should be a female, but not be over
30 years old.

You are requested to screen candidates and provide three
persons for me to interview for the position. Please do
this immediately. I will then let you know the name of
the candidate chosen for the position. Do not mention
the starting salary. Thank you for the outstanding service that you have provided in the past.

ri

M E M O R A N D U M

TO: Ada Jane Walters, Director
          Personnel Services

FROM: Bret R. Canty, Manager
          Office Support Services

DATE: Current Date

SUBJECT: Employment Needs

There is an <u>anticipated</u> opening in the office support
services area for <u>next</u> month.

A vacancy resulted after one of our employees, Robert ∧J.
Fults, was promoted to the Microcomputer Technical Resources Department to fill an opening in that area.
~~Robert has been in our department for almost two years.~~
Prospective candidates for the position should be able
to keyboard a <u>minimum</u> of 250 keystrokes per minute or
7,500 keystrokes during a 30-minute timing. A minimum
of two years of college is ∧the ~~required as an~~ /educational
requirement. The starting salary will be / $32,000

(An accuracy rate of 98 percent is required)   the names of
You are requested to screen candidates and ∧to provide ∧three
persons for me to interview ~~for the position.~~ ~~Please do
this immediately?~~ I will ~~then~~ let you know the name of
the candidate chosen for the position. ~~Do not mention
the starting salary?~~ Thank you for the **outstanding**
service that you have provided in the past.

ri

Application 3 Letter

Hint

Review the proofreading symbol guide on pages 141-142.

Hint

Use your spelling checker on all documents you create.

1. Key the letter shown in Example A using the default format of your word processing program. Use the underscore feature to create the form within the letter. If you are using the Paradigm data disk, retrieve the ASCII file AEXER3 or the WordPerfect file PEXER3.

2. Check the spelling of "Colorodo" in the second paragraph. Correct the spelling, if appropriate.

3. In paragraph 3 underline the word "lowest" in the first sentence. Boldface the words "We do vacations right" in the fourth sentence. Underline the words "happy" and "satisfied" in the fifth sentence.

4. Save the file as EXER3.

5. Print one copy of the letter.

6. Mrs. Rodriquez has marked changes on your first printed copy of the letter. Retrieve the file EXER3 and make the revisions shown in Example B.

7. Print one copy of the revised letter.

8. Save the revised document as EXER3.

Complete the entire exercise before answering the review questions.

1. What does the proofreading symbol # indicate?_____
   _____

2. Did you copy the form from the letter to the bottom of the page
   by blocking the form first? What keystroke sequence did you
   use?_____

3. What sequence of steps did you use to move the second text
   paragraph to the end of the letter?_____
   _____

4. What is the quickest way to delete the two sentences in the
   third paragraph? _____
   _____

   _____

5. Why was there a need to add space between Name, Address,
   and City/State/ZIP on the form portion? _____
   _____

   _____

Example A

Current Date

Mr. Frederick Nelson
9005 Frost Street
San Diego, CA 92120

Dear Mr. Nelson:

Thank you for inquiring about the availability of our WinterMont Snow Ski vacation package. You should include your
name and address in the following format:

Name _____
Address _____
City/State/ZIP _____

This form is repeated at the bottom of this letter to make
your reply as easy as possible. I look forward to working
with you to provide your family with a happy vacation in
Colorodo.

Our travel agency can provide you with the lowest vacation
package possible due to discounts based on our volume of
business with the leading ski resorts. Good values and low
prices make a combination that is hard to beat. Our travel
agency has served the San Diego area for over 20 years. We
do vacations right is a motto that is well earned. I want
to count you among our happy and satisfied vacationers. You
can be sure of getting the lowest price and best value possible due to volume discounts (which are passed on to our
clients) from vacation resorts around the country.

                    Sincerely,

                    (Mrs.) Amanda E. Rodriguez
                    Travel Consultant

ri

                    Clip and Return

- -

Example B

Current Date

Mr. Frederick Nelson
9005 Frost Street
San Diego, CA 92120

Dear Mr. Nelson:

Thank you for inquiring about ~~the availability of~~ our
[*Please*]
WinterMont Snow Ski vacation package. ~~You should~~ include
your name and address in the following format:

[*Copy this form to the bottom of the letter.*]

Name _____
  Address _____
City/State/ZIP _____

This form is repeated at the bottom of this letter to
make your reply as easy as possible. I look forward to
[*Move to end of letter, as a paragraph by itself.*]
working with you to provide ~~your family with a happy~~
~~vacation in Colorado.~~
[*Your choice of a Colorado vacation was a good one.*]

Our travel agency can provide you with the lowest
vacation package possible due to discounts based on our
volume of business with the leading ski resorts. ~~Good~~
~~values and low prices make a combination that is hard to~~
~~beat. Our travel agency~~ has served the San Diego area
~~for over 20 years.~~ **We do vacations right** is a motto that
is well earned. I want to count you among our happy and
satisfied vacationers. You can be sure of getting the
lowest price and best value possible due to volume discounts (which are passed on to our clients) from vacation
resorts around the country.

Sincerely,

(Mrs.) Amanda E. Rodriguez
Travel Consultant

ri

Clip and Return

Application 4 **Customer List**

1. Key the customer list on the next page. Make all rough draft changes as indicated.

2. Boldface each of the attention notations.

3. Arrange the customer list in alphabetical order by company name. Renumber the list.

4. Save the revised document as EXER4.

5. Print two copies of the customer list.

Hint

Use a tab feature to align the periods for each number in the list.

Complete the entire exercise before answering the review questions.

Review

1. What keystroke sequence did you use to center the first two lines? _____

2. What keystroke sequence did you use to make the indicated lines end evenly at the right margin?

_____

3. Did you insert the correct date for distribution?

_____

4. What tab settings or features were needed to enter the addresses? _____

center in all caps

Client List —— #
McHenry Corporation — center

End each line flush with the right margin.

ts —

Developed by
Department of Mail Services
Distribute on Monday, (First Monday of next month)

ts —

1. Branson Corporation
   Attn: ~~Jerry R. Flynn~~ Beverley R. Gamble
   2387 College Parkway
   Riverdale, NY 10471

2. Marist and Associates
   Attn: Ava B. Marist
   5328 Sycamore Avenue
   Terre Haute, IN 47809

3. Tawfik Legal Services
   Attn: Barry M. Tawfik
   3761 Scenic Hills Drive
   Monterey, CA 93943

4. Dudley Microcomputer Systems
   Attn: Chandra R. Lopez
   9261 Sepulveda Boulevard
   Los Angeles, CA 90034

5. Futuristic Consultants, Inc.
   Attn: Dennis G. Sollenberger
   7329 Tappan Street
   Ann Arbor, MI 48109

6. Marks, Marks, and Martin
   Attn: Rebecca W. Marks
   3753 Flowering Peach Drive
   Gainesville, FL 32611

7. Rasch Data Communications
   Attn: Stanley R. Sweeney
   5811 Brookhaven Circle
   Teaneck, NJ 07666

8. ALCO, Inc.
   Attn: Marietta F. Dolan
   One DuPont Circle, East
   Lakewood, NJ 08701

9. Distinctive Office Design — Attn: Joan P. Davis
   4555 Mervis Street
   Pittsburg, PA 15260

10. Markus and Associates, Consultants
    Attn: James T. Markus
    4448 Crow Road
    Dallas, TX 75275

Application 5 **Newsletter**

1. Key the newsletter on the following page. Format the text with 2-inch left and right margins. Change your program's hyphenation feature to automatic so that the program hyphenates words for you. Make the indicated corrections.

2. The main heading is to be centered over the page. Boldface the subheadings "Hardware" and "Software."

3. Proofread the newsletter for spelling and punctuation errors. (Use the spelling checker, if available.)

4. Save the file as EXER5.

5. Print one copy of the newsletter.

> Complete the entire exercise before answering the review questions.

Review

1. What are the advantages to adding additional line spaces on the page?_____

2. What keystroke sequence did you use to center the main heading?_____

Typical Microcomputer Products

There are several new microcomputer products on the market that can help increase productivity and reduce operating expenses.

Hardware

Many current end-users are using the 80486 microchip with math co-processors. Speeds exceeding 50 MHz are common. Hard drives are common on most equipment, with sizes above 165 Mb common. Most monitors provide VGA color capability to show graphics in a more vivid format and to display more distinct design and layout. Printers are changing to meet the needs of office support activities. While dot matrix printers offer speed as a feature, many offices are moving to laser printers, which offer speed and excellent quality. Networks provide a vehicle for communications and sharing of hardware and software resources. There are several network designs that can be used to meet the needs and limitations of most offices.

Software

There are many software products on the market to improve efficiency, but the standard packages such as word processing, spreadsheet, data base, and graphics remain dominant in the market. However, newer versions of these packages are constantly appearing.

Word processing software remains a staple in the office due to the widespread use of text applications and the ease of use of these programs with microcomputers. These programs can be used with networks and communications programs to facilitate transfer of information between users.

Spreadsheet software has many applications in the office and financial environments. Many types of software will permit spreadsheets to be imported into word processing documents.

Data base software can be used for inventory, mailing lists, and many other types of applications.

Graphics software can be used to present numeric data in a graphic format. *a word processing application*

Integrated software can be used in instances where there is a need to have ~~one type of software~~ relate to ~~another type of software,~~ such as producing a graph or table that will be later used in a letter.
a spreadsheet application

Microcomputer applications and needed equipment are likely to become much more sophisticated in the future. Good jobs will go to personnel who can effectively utilize microcomputers to perform office activities.

Application 6 **Letter**

1. Key the letter on the following page. Align the date and the complimentary closing.

2. Use a telephone directory to locate the area codes for the cities included in the letter. Include the area codes in the letter.

3. After you have keyed the letter, change the line length to 10 spaces (approximately one inch) less than was used for the original letter. Reformat the text (adjust the lines) to reflect the new margins. Proofread the letter for any changes made necessary by the new margins.

4. Save the file as EXER6.

5. Print one copy of the letter.

> Complete the entire exercise before answering the review questions.

Review

1. Where did you set a tab for the paragraph indention?

   _____

2. What tabs did you set for the city and the telephone area code columns? _____

3. What keystroke sequence did you use to align the date and the closing?_____

Current Date

Ms. Barbara Q. Mayberry
720 North Michigan Avenue
Chicago, IL 60611

Dear Ms. Mayberry:

   Welcome to our company as a marketing representative
for the Chicago area. Your service area will include the
cities with telephone area codes as indicated below.

            <u>City</u>   <u>Area Code</u>

      Chicago, Illinois
      St. Louis, Missouri
      Kansas City, Missouri
      Des Moines, Iowa

   I look forward to working with you and feel that you
have a bright future with our company.

                  Sincerely,

                  William J. Coombs, Director
                  Human Resources

ri

Name _____

Section _____ Date _____

Application 7 Sales Invoice

1. Key the following invoice. The invoice should appear on a single sheet of paper. Allocate enough space for the "Description." Long descriptions of the product may require two or more lines.

2. Use the underscore feature or the dash to create the horizontal lines and the ¦ symbol to draw the vertical lines.

3. Save the invoice as EXER7.

4. Print one copy of the invoice.

> Complete the entire exercise before answering the review questions.

Review

1. Some addresses may fill five full lines. What spacing is best for these lines to allow room to handwrite the address?

_____

2. You may want to review an accounting or business math textbook to locate examples of an invoice. Also, you may want to visit a merchandising business to secure examples of an invoice. What is the purpose of an invoice?

_____

_____

3. Did you consider using different fonts for different parts of the invoice to make it more attractive, if your software and printer offer more than one font? What font(s) are available with your software? _____

4. Did you use tabs to align the blank lines for "SOLD TO" and "Amount Due"? _____

Modern Office Supply
518 Americana Court
Des Moines, IA 50314

Invoice No. _____

SOLD TO _____

_____

_____

_____

_____

Item	Quantity	Description	Unit Price	Amount Due
		Total Sales:		_____
		Sales Tax (4 percent):		_____
		Total Amount Due:		_____

Thank you. Please pay by invoice. No statement will be sent.

Name _____

Section _____ Date _____

Application 8 **Customer List**

1. Retrieve the file EXER4. If you did not complete that application, retrieve the ASCII file AEXER8 or the WordPerfect file PEXER8 from the Paradigm data disk.

2. Make the revisions shown below so that the list fits on one page. Print the list.

3. Organize the addresses into two columns of equal length. (You may need to adjust the margins.) Add line spaces above the first address to center the data vertically on the page. An alternative is to print the entire listing as one column and then cut (with scissors) and paste the listings into two columns on a standard sheet of paper. You could then photocopy the page to produce a "clean" copy.

4. Save the file as EXER8.

5. Print two copies of the listing.

> Complete the entire exercise before answering the review questions.

Review

1. Did you change the margins of each column so the listings fit? What margins did you use? _____

2. What tab feature(s) did you use to create two columns?

   _____

3. Which list (one-column or two-column) is visually more appealing?_____

{ change top margin to .5"

CLIENT LIST

McHenry Corporation *} delete 1 line space*

Developed by
Department of Mail Services
Distribute on Monday, (First Monday of next month)

1. ALCO, Inc.
   Attn: Marietta F. Dolan
   One DuPont Circle, East
   Lakewood, NJ 08701

2. Branson Corporation
   Attn: Beverley R. Gamble
   2387 College Parkway
   Riverdale, NY 10471

3. Distinctive Office Design
   Attn: Joan P. Davis
   4555 Mervis Street
   Pittsburgh, PA 15260

4. Dudley Microcomputer Systems
   Attn: Chandra R. Lopez
   9261 Sepulveda Boulevard
   Los Angeles, CA 90034

5. Futuristic Consultants, Inc.
   Attn: Dennis G. Sollenberger
   7329 Tappan Street
   Ann Arbor, MI 48109

6. Marist and Associates
   Attn: Ava B. Marist
   5328 Sycamore Avenue
   Terre Haute, IN 47809

7. Marks, Marks, and Martin
   Attn: Rebecca W. Marks
   3753 Flowering Peach Drive
   Gainesville, FL 32611

8. Markus and Associates, Consultants
   Attn: James T. Markus
   4448 Crow Road
   Dallas, TX 75275

9. Rasch Data Communications
   Attn: Stanley R. Sweeney
   5811 Brookhaven Circle
   Teaneck, NJ 07666

10. Tawfik Legal Services
    Attn: Barry M. Tawfik
    3761 Scenic Hills Drive
    Monterey, CA 93943

Name _____

Section _____ Date _____

Application 9 **Letter Template**

1. Retrieve the file EXER1. If you did not complete that application, retrieve the ASCII file AEXER9 or the WordPerfect file PEXER9 from the Paradigm data disk. Make the rough-draft changes as indicated.

2. Replace the second paragraph in the letter with the itemized listing. Five items are included in the list. Add a sixth item that you feel is appropriate, based on the text of the letter. Center the list and align each number and the first letter of each entry.

3. Reverse the sentences in the last paragraph—the first sentence will become the last sentence and vice versa.

4. Print one copy of the revised letter.

5. Save the revised letter as EXER9.

> Complete the entire exercise before answering the review questions.

Review

1. Did you remember to change the salutation to reflect the new name? Why is Dr. more appropriate than Ms. for the title in the salutation?_____

2. Did you use a block feature to delete the second paragraph? What keystroke sequence did you use?

   _____

3. What keystroke sequence did you use to align the list of six advantages?_____

4. What feature or command did you use to reverse the order of the two sentences in the last paragraph? _____

Current Date

Mr. John R. Billings   *Dr. Rhonda A. DeWitt*   *Benefits in*
913 Coleman Avenue   *343 Linn Drive*   *attending the*
Atlanta, GA 30354   *Montclair, NJ 07044*   *seminar*
                                                        are listed
Dear Mr. Billings: *below.*

Thank you for inquiring about the **Time Management Seminar**
that will be located in your city in a few weeks.

The seminar will provide many ideas that will be helpful
as you complete your work and improve efficiency while you
perform office tasks. You will find ways to work **faster**
and complete more activities in a shorter period of time.
This will permit you to work in an environment where time
is used efficiently.

This six-hour seminar will help **save time** to help you and
others increase productivity in your Atlanta office. The
enclosed brochure provides additional information about
this seminar.
                                      Montclair

Sincerely,

Sarah W. Craig, Director
Professional Development Programs

>ri
Enclosure

1. Helpful ideas.
2. Efficiency improvement.
3. Faster work.
4. More activities.
5. Time management.
6.

Application 10 **Sales Invoice Template**

1. Key the following invoices using the invoice template you created in the file EXER7. If you did not complete that application, retrieve the ASCII file AEXER10 or the WordPerfect file PEXER10 from the Paradigm data disk.

2. The extensions and totals have been completed for Invoice No. 11023. Check the computations to insure that the amounts are accurate. Compute the extensions and totals for Invoice No. 11024 in the following order: (1) compute each extension; (2) compute the total sales amount; (3) compute the sales tax amount; and (4) compute the total amount due.

3. Print one copy of each of the invoices.

4. Save the files as EXER10-1 and EXER10-2.

> Complete the entire exercise before answering the review questions.

Review

1. Where should the tabs be set to permit entering of the data for the invoice? _____

2. What is the amount due for the 150 watt power supply units for the first item on Invoice No. 11024? _____

3. What happens if you use returns and the space bar instead of the cursor control keys to move to various locations in the invoice to make entries?_____

Modern Office Supply
518 Americana Court
Des Moines, IA 50314

Invoice No. 11023

SOLD TO Bryant, Carie and Associates

Attn: Deanna Canty

605 Bullard Avenue

New Orleans, LA 70128

Item	Quantity	Description	Unit Price	Amount Due
RX-1	24	RX-74 Printer Ribbons	1.89	45.36
2	36	8.5" x 11" Paper Packs for Laser Printer	3.49	125.64
3	8	Laser Printer Toner Packets - LA 2861	89.95	719.60
4	36	5.25" diskettes DSDD	0.79	28.44
5	42	3.5" diskettes MF2-HD	1.29	54.18

		Total Sales:		970.22
		Sales Tax (4 percent):		38.81
		Total Amount Due:		1,009.03

Thank you. Please pay by invoice. No statement will be sent.

Modern Office Supply
518 Americana Court
Des Moines, IA 50314

Invoice No. 11024

SOLD TO _City Community College_
Attn: Marilyn D. Austin
56 Eastern Promenade
Portland, ME 04101

Item	Quantity	Description	Unit Price	Amount Due
1	8	150 watt Power Supply for PC/AT	69.25	
2	15	Novelle Ethernet card	149.50	
3	12	GM-6X Serial Mouse	39.89	
4	6	80 Mb ST-4096 Drives	595.00	
5	12	2400 Baud Modem, ZX 143	84.50	
		Total Sales:		_____
		Sales Tax (4 percent):		_____
		Total Amount Due:		_____

Thank you. Please pay by invoice. No statement will be sent.

Application 11 **Unit Mastery**

You are working as a word processing specialist in the office of Human Resources. Ralph A. Marshall, Director of Professional Development Seminars, asks you to prepare a letter to be sent to persons requesting information about seminars. After you prepare a draft of the letter, Mr. Marshall edits it and you must incorporate those changes into the final copy.

Mr. Marshall also wants you to develop a form that can be used to gather information from respondents who have indicated an interest in the proposed seminars.

1. Key the letter shown in Example A. This represents the transcription of a letter dictated on tape by Mr. Marshall. If you are using the Paradigm data disk, retrieve the ASCII file AEXER11, or the WordPerfect file PEXER11.

2. Boldface both instances of the words "low cost" in the second paragraph. Underline the words "next few weeks" in the second paragraph.

3. Check the spelling of the entire document.

4. Save the file as EXER11.

5. Print one copy of the letter.

6. Mr. Marshall has read the letter you have prepared and has marked several changes. Make the revisions shown in Example B. Add an enclosure notation for the form that will be sent with the letter.

7. Save the revised letter as EXER11 and print a copy.

8. Prepare the form shown in Example C. It is to be enclosed with the letter.

9. Print one copy of the form.

10. Save the form as EXER11-2.

Example A

Current Date

Ms. Sarah P. Lancaster
Chief Operating Officer
Automated Data Systems, Inc.
601 Hudson Avenue
Albany, NY 12203

Dear Ms. Lancaster:

Thank you for requesting information about the possibility of
our offering seminars in your area in the near future. We
realize that you are in need of this type of training.

Professional development seminars are a way to upgrade employee skills at a low cost. You and your employees can attend the seminars at a surprisingly low cost. I look forward
to hearing from you soon. Our team will arrive in Missisippi
within the next few weeks and will be happy to arrange to
visit with you to offer a seminar for your employees.

Please let me know if you have questions or need additional
information about our professional development seminars.

Sincerely,

Ralph A. Marshall, Director
Professional Development Seminars

ri

Example B

Current Date

Ms. Sarah P. ~~Lancaster~~ *Murphy*
Chief Operating Officer
Automated Data Systems, Inc.
601 Hudson Avenue
Albany, NY 12203
Dear Ms. ~~Lancaster:~~ *Murphy:*

Thank you for requesting information about ~~the possibility of our offering~~ *(being offered)* seminars in your area ~~in the near future. We realize that you are in need of this type of training.~~

(Benefits are listed below.)

Professional development seminars are a way to upgrade employee skills at a **low cost.** ~~You and your employees can attend the seminars at a surprisingly low cost.~~ *(I look forward to hearing from you soon.)* ~~Our team will arrive in Mississippi within the next few weeks and will be happy to arrange to visit with you to offer a~~ seminar for your ~~employees.~~

~~Please let me know if you have questions or need additional information about our professional development seminars.~~

Sincerely,

Please complete the enclosed form to let me know about how many of your employees will attend the seminar.

Ralph A. Marshall, Director
Professional Development Seminars

ri

1. Low Cost
2. (Improvement of Morale)
3. Excellent Instruction
4. Time Used Wisely

Example C

```
                      Seminar Registration Form


Names of Seminars Needed:     _____

Number of Employees
Who Will Attend:              _____

Company Name and Address:     _____

                             _____

                             _____

                             _____


Person to Contact:            _____

Phone Number:                 _____

Best Time of Day to Call:     _____


Please return to: Mr. Ralph A. Marshall, Director
                  Professional Development Seminars
                  Executive Seminars Unlimited
                  178 Diamond Road
                  Minneapolis, MN 56804
```

Unit 2

Page Formatting

Applications 12, 13, and 14 include page formatting features such as search and replace, special font pitches and types, and variable line lengths. Unique applications such as a passenger list, an invitation to a reception, and a newspaper advertisement are used for these exercises. A journal advertisement is presented in Application 15 to permit more extensive use of column layout and page format design.

Applications 16 and 17 require using superscripts, research footnotes, and hard page breaks. Software functions relating to verification of spelling and choosing alternate words are illustrated in Application 18. Application 19 offers an opportunity to design a letterhead for a document. Alignment of decimal values is the focus of Application 20.

In the remaining applications, previously stored documents and a simulation provide realistic examples for practicing many of the new functions presented in this unit.

Application 12 **Passenger List**

1. Key the passenger list on the next page. This list will be used to determine flight schedules for employees going to a conference in California.

2. Center the title on the page in all capital letters.

3. Use your software's search function to determine the flight schedule for Blanche W. Carter. What time is she leaving?

   _____

4. Use a search function to determine the flight schedule for George A. Waggoner. What is his flight number? _____

5. Use a search function to determine the flight schedule for Roberta E. Tollerson. What is her flight number? _____

6. Use a search function to find names of employees who will be on flight 311. How many are on this flight? _____

7. Use your software's replace function to change the flight numbers for all employees on flight 311 to flight 375.

8. Use your replace function to change the name of Blanche W. Carter to Blanche W. Boyle.

9. Use your search function to determine the names of employees who will be on flight 375. How many are on this flight?

   _____

10. Are the numbers of employees obtained in numbers 6 and 9 the same? _____

11. Save the file as EXER12.

12. Print one copy of the passenger list.

> Complete the entire exercise before answering the review questions.

Review

1. What are the keystrokes you used to find Blanche W. Carter's time of departure? _____

2. What are the keystrokes you used to change "Carter" to "Boyle"?

   _____

Passenger List

John A. Billings, flight 311, leaving @ 4:15 P.M.
Martin P. Dole, flight 416, leaving @ 3:20 P.M.
Carol E. Jensen, flight 311, leaving @ 4:15 P.M.
Roberta E. Tollerson, flight 719, leaving at 2:35 P.M.
Ronald R. Powell, flight 416, leaving at 3:20 P.M.
Brenda C. Donaldson, flight 919, leaving at 10:45 A.M.
Frans Mueller, flight 311, leaving @ 4:15 P.M.
Roy T. Dickerson, flight 416, leaving @ 3:20 P.M.
Blanche W. Carter, flight 719, leaving @ 2:35 P.M.
Donald U. Reese, flight 416, leaving @ 3:20 P.M.
Clarence T. Maze, flight 919, leaving @ 10:45 A.M.
George A. Waggoner, flight 311, leaving @ 4:15 P.M.
Harry Rivera, flight 808, leaving @ 2:00 P.M.
John Montovan, flight 890, leaving @ 6:15 A.M.
Jeri Peters, flight 111, leaving @ 9:14 P.M.
Ellen Michaels, flight 114, leaving @ 7:35 P.M.
Jill Larson, flight 018, leaving @ 5:34 P.M.
Russ Lewis, flight 027, leaving @ 3:15 P.M.
Sean Cooper, flight 298, leaving @ 9:20 P.M.
Marc Lucas, flight 271, leaving @ 8:45 P.M.
Joan Orlando, flight 178, leaving @ 1:15 P.M.
Teresa Felland, flight 114, leaving @ 6:05 P.M.
Kelsey Romero, flight 277, leaving @ 4:00 P.M.
Megan Lancaster, flight 298, leaving @ 9:20 P.M.

Name _____

Section _____ Date _____

Application 13 **Invitation**

1. Key the invitation on the next page. Make the indicated corrections. If your software permits, use different font sizes (three) for different parts of the invitation.

2. Center each line horizontally, except for the last line, which will begin at the left margin.

3. Center the invitation vertically on the page. You may assume that a half sheet of standard-size paper (8 1/2" x 11") is being used.

4. Make the date correspond with the first Monday of next month.

5. Save the file as EXER13.

6. Print one copy of the invitation.

> Complete the entire exercise before answering the review questions.

Review

1. Check the font sizes and designs that are available with your software. Print a few to determine how they appear on the printed page. Which fonts are available with your software?

   _____

   _____

2. Which fonts and sizes did you select as the most appropriate for the party invitation? Why? _____

   _____

3. How many lines are available on the half sheet of paper?___
   How many lines will be used for the invitation?_____
   How many lines from the top should the first line appear?__

4. What other features can be added to give the invitation an attractive design? _____

   _____

                                    All
Party Invitation to ᴧEmployees
            Participation
Your ~~Attendance~~ is Requested at the

Annual Founder's Day Reception

Date

at 6:30 P.M. ~~in the Evening~~

President's Conference Hall
                    Will
Refreshments ~~to~~ be Served

RSVP

Application 14 **Help Wanted Ad**

1. Retrieve the ASCII file AEXER14 or the WordPerfect file PEXER14 from the Paradigm data disk.

2. Make the changes as indicated on the following page (as your software permits).

3. Check with other members of your class or local businesses to determine an appropriate keying speed and salary amount for entry-level administrative assistants in your area. What speed did you consider to be appropriate? _____ What salary amount did you consider to be appropriate? _____ Make the appropriate changes in the ad.

4. Save the file as EXER14.

5. Print one copy of the help wanted ad.

Complete the entire exercise before answering the review questions.

Review

1. Did you format the "Equal Opportunity Employer" notation in italics, if supported by your software, or in boldface type otherwise? _____

2. What is the purpose of the "Equal Opportunity Employer" notation? _____

ADMINISTRATIVE ASSISTANT

~~East office of~~ national insurance firm seeks
experienced administrative assistant with
excellent secretarial skills including
training with microcomputers and WordPerfect
or ~~other~~ comparable software program. Key-
boarding skills of 50 WPM required. Must be *excellent*
exceptionally well organized with ~~good~~ com-
munication skills and a professional appearance. ∧ Competitive salary and excellent
fringe benefits. Send resume to ~~Box 4789.~~
and salary requirements

Equal Opportunity Employer

italics

Nonsmoking work environment.

National Insurance Agency,
2760 Starnes Cove, Memphis,
TN 38116.

Application 15 Journal Advertisement

1. Key the following journal advertisement. Make all rough draft changes as indicated.

2. Format the "Product Features" section into two columns if your software permits. (Otherwise, print the features in one column. Then use scissors to divide the column in half and paste on the page.)

3. If your software permits, use a graphics feature to produce the bullet at the beginning of each "Product Feature." Otherwise, use a period.

4. Proofread the document and save the file as EXER15.

5. Print three copies of the advertisement.

Complete the entire exercise before answering the review questions.

Review

1. Why is the compatibility of a product with Lotus 1-2-3 or dBASE considered to be an important feature? _____

   _____

   _____

2. How could you format the "Product Features" heading to make it stand out? _____

   _____

3. Did you add the lines needed to make the two columns begin on the same line so they are approximately equal in length?

   _____

Top Choice Accounting Software *center in all caps*
New Version 7.11 Ready Now *center*

<u>Top Choice Accounting Software</u>, version 7.11, is ready for immediate shipment. This software, ~~already~~ preferred by over 30 percent of small business owners, will appeal to corporate groups due to the new version's compatib~~le~~*ility* with popular products such as Lotus® 1-2-3® and dBASE®.

A unique modular approach permits you to fit the product ~~exactly~~ to your needs. You save because only the modules needed for ~~your~~ specific applications have to be purchased. ~~Other~~ modules can be added later as you grow and/or your needs change. Authorized support centers are located in 8~~7~~5 cities across the country.

This amazing product's price has been reduced to $279, when purchased in quantities of five or more copies. Call now to order. For a dealer nearest you, call 1-800-555-3271. To order by fax, call 1-800-555-3272.

Product Features

boldface
General Ledger
·Up to 25,000 accounts
·Comparative financial
    statements
·Adjustments for prior periods
Accounts Payable *boldface*
·Invoice partial payments
·Check printing
·Prints misc. 1099s
Accounts Receivable *boldface*
·Balance forward
·Open item accounting
·Maintains address file
Purchasing *boldface*
·Updates purchase orders
·Updates inventory
·Generates A/P invoices from
    purchase order
Payroll *boldface*
·Up to 15,000 employees
·Accrues sick and vacation
    time
·Prints checks and W-2s
·Calculates payroll taxes
·Determines deductions

boldface
Inventory
·Supports LIFO, FIFO, Spe-
    cific Unit, standard and
    average costing methods
·Up to 15,000 inventory items
·Serial number tracking
Fixed Assets *boldface*
·Up to 15,000 items
·Handles 13 methods of
    depreciation
Reports *boldface*
·Custom and predefined report
    formats
·Support line and bar graph
    data representation
·Transfer data to Lotus® 1-2-3®
    and dBASE®.

Note: Lotus 1-2-3 is a registered trademark of Lotus Development Corporation. dBASE
is a registered trademark of
Ashton-Tate Corporation.

Use a smaller font size for this note.

Application 16 Report

1. Key the following report. The body of the report should be double-spaced. Justify the text so that all lines line up at the left and right margins. Check the spelling of "transpariences" to make sure that the word is spelled correctly. Correct, if needed. If your software permits, check the spelling throughout the report.

2. The footnotes should be single-spaced, with a double space after each footnote if more than one footnote appears on a page. Space the footnotes so that the last line of the last footnote is 1 inch from the bottom of the page.

3. Footnote notations should be raised, as shown in the report. These are called superscripts. If your software and/or printer do not support this feature, the footnote notation should be enclosed in brackets as follows: [1].

4. If the report requires more than one page, number the pages. Center the page number at the bottom of the page.

5. Save the file as EXER16.

6. Print one copy of the report.

Complete the entire exercise before answering the review questions.

1. What coding or functions are necessary to print raised foot-note notations (superscripts)? _____

   _____

2. Did you create a line, 1.5 inches long, to separate the body from the footnotes?_____

3. Did you triple-space before and double-space after each sub-heading?_____

4. The footnote reference should appear on the same page as the notation in this report. Note: Some footnote styles permit you to include all footnotes at the end of the report—as opposed to the bottom of the page. Does this method make keying a long report easier? Why?

   _____

   _____

   _____

   _____

   _____

   _____

ts

ds ——— There are several important items that should be considered prior to the purchase of a graphics package.

ts
Charting

ds

ds One secret to buying a graphics package is to select one that permits selecting the right chart for the data.[1] Good packages support mixed graphs (bars and lines), three-dimensional, scatterplots, and stock market graphs, as well as the usual bar, column, line, and pie charts.

ts
Enhancement

ds

ds The ability to add color is an important feature. The ability to edit the graph as well as rotate and flip objects is also important. Clip-art libraries are also important to permit the user to import graphic designs.

ts
Presentation Controls

ds

ds The ability to modify colors and fonts globally is important. It is also helpful to be able to print a copy of the slide, which can then be used as a handout while the graph is being displayed. For the sake of readability, the program should also be able to convert colors to appropriate black-and-white shades and patterns.

ts
Output

ds

ds The largest criterion of any graphics package is its finished output.[2] The package should support a full range of printers and plotters. Support for 35mm slides and color transpariencies is also important.

ts
Final Note

ds

ds There are a number of high-quality graphics software programs that meet these four criteria. The emphasis on graphics is expected to increase dramatically during the next decade.

---

[1]Robert T. Pollard, "Graphic Software Selection," _Journal of Graphic Design_, vol. 34, no. 2 (April 1991), 35.

[2]Brenda E. Johnson, "Evaluating Presentation Products," _Presentation Products Unlimited_, vol. 8, no. 5 (May 1991).

Application 17 **Outline**

1. Key the following partial outline including the editing changes. Double-space the outline.

2. Create a page break so that each of the three sections appears on a separate page.

3. Prepare a "header" so that the words "Return to Room 1411" appear on each page.

4. Set 5-space tabs to indent lines five spaces.

5. Save the file as EXER17.

6. Print one copy of the outline.

> Complete the entire exercise before answering the review questions.

Review

1. What coding sequence did you use to create a hard page break?

   _____

   _____

2. What coding sequence did you use to print the header?

   _____

   _____

3. Did you use tabs to align the chapter titles as well as the unit titles?_____

COLLEGE BUSINESS MATHEMATICS (Brief Course)

⑤ Unit 1 - (Basic Mathematical Operations) *boldface*
   ⑤ Chapter 1 - Accurate Addition
      Chapter 2 - Subtraction, Multiplication, and Division
      Chapter 3 - Merchandising Records
      Chapter 4 - Reconciling a Bank Statement
      Chapter 5 - Information Processing
      Unit 1 Self-Test

Unit 2 - (Decimals) *boldface*
      Chapter 6 - Decimals: An Overview
      Chapter 7 - Decimals: Addition and Subtraction
      Chapter 8 - Decimals: Multiplication and Division
      Unit 2 Spreadsheet Applications
      Unit 2 Self-Test

Unit 3 - (Percentage in Business) *boldface*
      Chapter 9 - Using an Electronic Calculator
      Chapter 10 - Percentage Amounts in Business
      Chapter 11 - Base and Rate Applications
      Chapter 12 - Finance Charges
      Chapter 13 - Discounts on Purchases
      Unit 3 Spreadsheet Applications
      Unit 3 Self-Test

Application 18 Letter

1. Retrieve the ASCII file AEXER18 or the WordPerfect file PEXER18 from the Paradigm data disk.

2. Make the changes indicated in the following copy.

3. Use your spelling checker or a dictionary (if spelling checker is unavailable), to check the spelling throughout the letter. Proofread the letter for errors the spelling checker cannot find.

4. A form of the word "select" was used two times in the first paragraph. The word "process" is also used two times in the first paragraph. Use the thesaurus feature, if available, to determine alternatives for these words.

5. Save the corrected file as EXER18.

6. Print one copy of the revised letter.

> Complete the entire exercise before answering the review questions.

Review

1. If you used a spelling checker, did you choose to check the page or the document?_____

2. Did the spelling checker indicate double words?_____

   Note: The word "bid" appeared twice in the first sentence, and the word "to" was doubled in the second paragraph.

3. What kinds of spelling errors are not detected by a spelling checker? _____

Current Date

Mr. Thomas A. Bettinger, President
Dover Electronics, International
5600 North Lindsay Street
Oklahoma City, OK 73190

Dear Mr. Bettinger:

Thank yu for selecting our company to bid bid on your anticipated purchase of office equipmint and ~~office~~ furni-
ture. Our bid process will follow the process that you
outlined for the merchandise selection.

~~Miss~~ Joan G. Merriweather, Regional Manager serving the
Oklahoma City area, will providde you with a response to
your recent request for bids. Since her office serves
you area, providing products to to your ~~area~~ will be much
fasterr. Therefour, I feel that our company can provide
your with the (best service possible) at the (lowest cost
possible).
                                            boldface
                        Ms.
You will hear from ~~Miss~~ Merriweather in a few days. In
the meantime, please let me know if you have questons or
nead additional information.

Sincerely,

John T. Malloy, Manager
National Accounts

ri

c: Joan G. Merriweather

Application 19 Letterhead

1. Key a letterhead memo that includes the following information. Obtain copies of letterheads used by businesses in your area. Base your design on the best features and layout of each letterhead.

2. Use fonts, if available with your software, to make the letterhead more attractive. Otherwise, use regular fonts.

3. Set tabs at the places where the user will enter the following information: TO, FROM, DATE, and SUBJECT.

4. Save the file as EXER19.

5. Print one copy of the letterhead memo.

> Complete the entire exercise before answering the review questions.

Review

1. Where did you decide that the tab stops should appear?

   _____

2. Review the Memphis State University letterhead shown on page 55. What suggestions do you have for improving or changing this letterhead?_____

<u>Information to Be Included on the Letterhead</u>

Note: The company can use the same form for letters
except the notations for TO, FROM, DATE, and SUBJECT
will be removed. Other companies prefer to simply have
the title "MEMORANDUM" at the top without the company
name, address, and so forth.

Company Name: Garner and Associates
Street Address: 1400 Aldrich Avenue S.
City/State/ZIP: Minneapolis, MN 55420
Telephone Number: (612) 555-7241
Special Notation: An Equal Opportunity Employer
Graphic: Optional, depending on software and your de-
sign
Motto: The Client Comes First

(901) 555-2462

TO:

FROM:

DATE:

SUBJECT:

Management Information Systems and Decision Sciences Department
300 Fogelman College of Business and Economics/Memphis, Tennessee 38152

An Equal Opportunity/Affirmative Action University

Letterhead • 55

Application 20 **Table**

---

1. Key the following table. Include all the rough draft changes.

2. Decide on appropriate distances between columns so that the table is attractive.

3. Make the date, in the secondary heading, the last day of the past month. Use a calculator to compute the total of the Monthly Pay. Place this amount in the appropriate place at the bottom of the column.

4. Save the file as EXER20.

5. Print one copy of the table.

> Complete the entire exercise before answering the review questions.

Review

1. What did you choose for the distance between columns?

_____

2. Did you use both regular and decimal tabs to format the table?

_____

<u>Payroll Report</u>

ds

For the Month Ending —

ts

Employee No.	Department	Monthly Pay
ds		
456-23-43(29)	Sales	2,456.83
532-34-2643	~~Sales~~ Production	2,145.56
023-34-5329	Sales	2,500.89
154-34-2592	Production	3,105.78
021-45-3501	Management	2,750.50
108-45-2812	~~Production~~ Sales	2,108.38
054-83-8271	Sales	~~2,141.89~~ 3,007.42
724-45-8908	Management	2,676.85
183-73-0199	Management	2,105.52
076-38-5328	Production	<u>2,045.90</u>

Total:

Application 21 **Passenger List Template**

1. Retrieve file EXER12 created in Application 12. If you did not complete that application, retrieve the ASCII file AEXER21 or the WordPerfect file PEXER21 from the Paradigm data disk. The passenger list created in that file also appears below for your reference.

2. The passenger list will be more readable if it is placed in table format. Rearrange the data in the table into three columns, with column headings. What names appear to be appropriate for the three columns? _____
_____

3. Instead of keying the table again, insert tabs. Then delete information that is not needed in the column since it shows in the column heading—such as the word "Flight."

4. Save the file as EXER21.

5. Print one copy of the table.

> Complete the entire exercise before answering the review questions.

Review

1. Did you remember to delete the commas and other unnecessary information in the table?_____

2. Did you center the data under column headings?_____

3. Did you review the table for accuracy?_____

PASSENGER LIST

John A. Billings, flight 375, leaving @ 4:15 P.M.
Martin P. Dole, flight 416, leaving @ 3:20 P.M.
Carol E. Jensen, flight 375, leaving @ 4:15 P.M.
Roberta E. Tollerson, flight 719, leaving at 2:35 P.M.
Ronald R. Powell, flight 416, leaving at 3:20 P.M.
Brenda C. Donaldson, flight 919, leaving at 10:45 A.M.
Frans Mueller, flight 375, leaving @ 4:15 P.M.
Roy T. Dickerson, flight 416, leaving @ 3:20 P.M.
Blanche W. Boyle, flight 719, leaving @ 2:35 P.M.
Donald U. Reese, flight 416, leaving @ 3:20 P.M.
Clarence T. Maze, flight 919, leaving @ 10:45 A.M.
George A. Waggoner, flight 375, leaving @ 4:15 P.M.
Harry S. Rivera, flight 808, leaving @ 2:00 P.M.
John P. Montovan, flight 890, leaving @ 6:15 A.M.
Jeri B. Peters, flight 111, leaving @ 9:14 P.M.
Ellen A. Michaels, flight 114, leaving @ 7:35 P.M.
Jill E. Larson, flight 018, leaving @ 5:34 P.M.
Russ L. Lewis, flight 027, leaving @ 3:15 P.M.
Sean F. Cooper, flight 298, leaving @ 9:20 P.M.
Marc P. Lucas, flight 271, leaving @ 8:45 P.M.
Joan N. Orlando, flight 178, leaving @ 1:15 P.M.
Teresa L. Felland, flight 114, leaving @ 6:05 P.M.
Kelsey J. Romero, flight 277, leaving @ 4:00 P.M.
Megan D. Lancaster, flight 298, leaving @ 9:20 P.M.

Application 22 **Report Template**

1. Retrieve the file EXER16, created in Application 16. If you did not complete that application, retrieve the ASCII file AEXER22 or the WordPerfect file PEXER22 from the Paradigm data disk.

2. Make the rough draft changes shown on the following pages.

3. Change the line length to 50 spaces.

4. After the report has been revised and reformatted to a 50-space line, make the adjustments necessary to include the footnotes on the correct page.

5. Save the file as EXER22.

6. Print two copies of the revised report.

> Complete the entire exercise before answering the review questions.

Review

1. Are the page numbers in the appropriate place on each page?
   _____

2. Some software programs reformat automatically after the line length has been changed. Does your software fall into this category?_____ If the answer is no, what steps did you take to reformat the document for a 50-space line? _____
   _____

   _____

3. Did you format the report so that the footnotes appear on the page where the source is referenced? _____

BUYING TIPS FOR GRAPHICS PACKAGES

There are several important items that should be considered prior to the purchase of a graphics package. *This report discusses four primary areas that are important.*

Charting

One secret to buying a graphics package is to select one that permits selecting the right chart for the data.[1] Good packages support mixed graphs (bars and lines), three-dimensional, scatterplots, and stock market graphs, as well as the usual bar, column, line, and pie charts.[2]

Enhancement

The ability to add color is *another* ~~an~~ important feature. The ability to edit the graph, as well as rotate and flip objects, is also *significant?* ~~important.~~ Clip-art libraries are also important to permit the user to import graphic designs.

Presentation Controls

The ability to modify colors and fonts globally is important. It is also helpful to be able to print a copy of the slide, which can then be used as a handout while the graph is being displayed. For the sake of readability, the program should also be able to convert colors to appropriate black-and-white shades and patterns.

---

[1]Robert T. Pollard, "Graphic Software Selection," *Journal of Graphic Design*, vol. 34, no. 2 (April 1991): 35.

[2]*Brenda A. Jones, "Graphic Packages," Journal of Graphic Design, vol. 34, no. 3 (May 1991): 16.*

Output

The largest criterion of any graphics package is its finished output.³ The package should support a full range of printers and plotters. Support for 35mm slides and color transparencies is also important.

Final Note

There are a number of high-quality graphics software programs that meet these four criteria. The emphasis on graphics is expected to increase dramatically during the next decade.

---

3 Brenda E. Johnson, "Evaluating Presentation Products," _Presentation Products Unlimited_, vol. 8, no. 5 (May 1991): 29.

Application 23 **Letterhead Template**

Text can be blocked and moved to save keyboarding time and reduce errors.	1. Retrieve the letterhead file EXER19 created in Application 19. If you did not complete that application, retrieve the ASCII file AEXER23 or the WordPerfect file PEXER23 from the Paradigm data disk.

2. Use the memo format to send the message in Example A (including the changes) announcing a new printer product. Note that the appearance of the letterhead will be different from the one shown if you are using the letterhead from Application 19.

3. Save the file as EXER23.

4. Print one copy of the completed memorandum.

5. Your boss, Ms. Toole, has asked you to revise the memo and send it as a letter. Retrieve the file EXER23.

6. Make the changes indicated in Example B. Save the file as EXER23-1.

7. Print <u>two</u> copies of the letter.

> Complete the entire exercise before answering the review questions.

Review

1. Did you include a double space before and after the salutation in the letter?_____

2. Did you leave 3 blank lines following the complimentary closing (Sincerely,)?_____

Example A

Garner and Associates
1400 Aldrich Avenue S.
Minneapolis, MN 55420

(612) 555-7241   The Client Comes First

TO: Office Support Staff

FROM: Donna Toole, Manager
           Office Information Systems

DATE: (Current Date)

SUBJECT: New Printer Update

Authorization has been requested to purchase ~~350~~ 425 of the new
PR9 Laser Printers. Plans are to have the printers in offices within 90 days.

One advantage of the new printers is that they can print
duplex, which will help save paper costs by printing long
reports on both sides of the page. Transparencies in black
and white can be prepared in various shades of black. This
will save money that has been previously used ~~by having
these~~ materials ~~prepared~~ to prepare on the plotter. Printing speed
will be eight pages per minute.

Please let me know within ~~30~~ 45 days ~~whether or not~~ if you ~~will~~ plan to
request one of the new printers. You should include justi-
fication, since I anticipate that more requests will be
recieved than printers are available.

ri

An Equal Opportunity Employer

Example B

Garner and Associates
1400 Aldrich Avenue S.
Minneapolis, MN 55420

(612) 555-7241   The Client Comes First

~~TO: Office Support Staff~~

~~FROM:~~   Donna Toole, Manager
         Office Information Systems

~~DATE:~~   (Current Date)

Mr. Donald R. Crum, President
national Media, Inc.
2106 marlton Pike
Cherry Hill, NH 08034
Dear mr. Crum:

~~SUBJECT: New Printer Update~~

Authorization has been requested to purchase ~~425 of the~~ new
PR9 Laser Printers. Plans are to have the printers in offices within 90 days.

One advantage of the new printers is that they can print duplex, which will help save paper costs by printing long reports on both sides of the page. Transparencies in black and
white can be prepared in various shades of black. This will
save money that has been previously used to prepare these
materials on the plotter. Printing speed will be eight pages
per minute.

                           whether or not
Please let me know within 45 days ~~if~~ you plan to request one
of the new printers. ~~You should include justification, since
I anticipate that more requests will be received than printers are available.~~ I will be happy to reserve one
~~for your office.~~
(ri)

Sincerely,

An Equal Opportunity Employer

Application 24 **Unit Mastery**

Document input arrives at your desk in many forms, including the handwritten format. Ms. Mable Burchfield, Director of Marketing Research, brings a handwritten letter to your desk with a request that it be prepared for a person requesting sales information from her office.

Electronic spreadsheets are very helpful for preparing reports that include numerical data. Ms. Burchfield requests that you include information, previously created in spreadsheet format, in the body of the letter you will prepare.

1. Prepare a letter from the information on the following page.

2. Use information from the spreadsheet on page 71 to prepare a table, which will be included in the letter with the following exception: include only the first four columns of the spreadsheet in the table. Otherwise, the format should be similar to the one in Application 20. Remember to center the data under the columns and to center the main headings.

3. Answer the following questions about the spreadsheet.
   a. Which region had the highest prior sales? _____
   b. Which region had the lowest current sales? _____
   c. Which region had the largest increase? _____
   d. How many regions had prior sales greater than the average amount? _____
   e. Which region had a decrease in sales during the current year? _____

4. Save the file as EXER24.

5. Print one copy of the letter containing the table.

(current date)

Mr. Elliot Perry, Supervisor
BGF Manufacturing Products, Inc.
2895 Southern Avenue
Memphis, TN 38111

Dear Mr. Perry:

Thank you for requesting information about our sales record this year.

The table[1] shown below provides data relative to sales last year, sales during the current year, and increase (or decrease). I have also included information about average, total, highest, and lowest amounts in _each_ category.

Insert data from spreadsheet →

This information will be included in our next Annual Report, due for publication in a few weeks. In the meantime, let me know if you have questions about the sales report.

Sincerely,

Mable Burchfield, Director
Marketing Research

[1] Annual Report Summary

```
           A          B          C              D                   E
 1  National Sales Report
 2  Bradford Motor Works
 3  (Sales Amounts Shown in Thousands)
 4  =========================================================================
 5  Sales         Prior      Current        Increase           Percent
 6  Region        Sales      Sales          (Decrease)         Change
 7  -------------------------------------------------------------------------
 8  Central       4,876      4,898                22             0.45%
 9  East          3,274      3,872               598            18.27%
10  North         3,729      3.529              (200)            -5.36%
11  South         4,121      4,238               117             2.84%
12  West          3,926      4,103               177             4.51%
13  -------------------------------------------------------------------------
14      Average:  3,985      4,128               143    xxxxxxxxxxxxxxx
15        Total: 19,926     20,640               714    xxxxxxxxxxxxxxx
16      Highest:  4,876      4,898               598    xxxxxxxxxxxxxxx
17       Lowest:  3,274      3,529              -200    xxxxxxxxxxxxxxx
18  =========================================================================
19
20
27-Oct-90 8:35 PM
```

Unit 3

Document Formatting

While one page was the normal length for documents created in previous units, some of the documents in Unit 3 will require more than one page. However, these multiple-page documents are fairly short. Many business reports include a cover page to give the reader vital information about the report. You will create this document in Application 25. The report's table of contents, to be completed in Application 26, provides a listing of topics and page numbers.

A multiple-page report is the focus of Application 27. Application 28 involves creating a bibliography, a list of the references cited in the report. You will create hanging indentions in this document. Working with a legal complaint will give you additional practice with multiple-page documents in Application 29.

Other types of documents featured in this unit include legal documents and form letters. Completing these applications requires developing boilerplates, revising text, merging addresses with form letters, and updating and reformatting stored files.

Application 25 **Report Cover Page**

1. Key the following report cover page.

2. Center each line. Arrange the lines so that the top and bottom sections are the same distance from the end of the page, with the middle section in the center of the page. Double-space the lines within each section.

3. Obtain copies of reports from your library and review their formats. Notice in particular the way that the title page, table of contents, footnotes (if any), and spacing are handled. Note that there are several formats suitable for reports.

4. Save the file as EXER25.

5. Print two copies of the report cover page.

> Complete the entire exercise before answering the review questions.

Review

1. How many blank lines did you leave at the top? _____

2. Did you leave an equal amount of space between the top and middle sections and between the middle and bottom sections?

   _____

3. Did you leave an equal amount of space at the top and bottom of the page? _____

4. What other design features could you use to make the cover page more attractive? _____

   _____

   _____

Mail Order Buying
Tips and Tricks

all caps

Prepared for
Mail Magazine Guide

by
Alfred R. Rosenburg
(Current Date)

Application 26 **Table of Contents**

---

1. Key the following table of contents. Include the rough draft changes.

2. Use a 1.5-inch left margin, a 1-inch right margin, a 1.5-inch top margin, and a 1-inch bottom margin (if the table of contents and page numbers fill the page). The page number should be a lowercase roman numeral ii centered 1 inch from the bottom of the page.

3. Use dot leaders (alternating periods and spaces) between each table of contents entry and its page number.

4. Notice that the last line of the table of contents refers to a bibliography. Review a dictionary or style manual to determine the purpose of a bibliography. You will learn how to prepare a bibliography in a later application. Many business reports do not include a bibliography. Why not? _____

_____

5. Save the file as EXER26.

6. Print one copy of the table of contents.

Complete the entire exercise before answering the review questions.

Review

1. Did you align the periods while keying the leaders? _____

2. Did you allow one space between each leader? _____

3. Notice that the page number for the table of contents is a lowercase roman numeral. Can you think of a reason for using different page number styles on the table of contents and the body of the report? _____

Table of Contents

center

Application 27 **Manuscript**

1. Key the manuscript on the following pages. Include all rough draft changes.

2. Use a 1.5-inch left margin, a 1-inch right margin, a 1-inch bottom margin, and a 1-inch top margin. Note: An exception is the first page, which will have a 1.5-inch top margin.

3. Center the page number on the first page 1 inch from the bottom. Number all other pages at the right margin 1 inch from the top of the page.

4. Double-space the text, including the headings.

5. Read the report carefully. Assuming that you plan to order a microcomputer system, what are five items that you deem important—ranked in order of importance?
   a. _____
   b. _____
   c. _____
   d. _____
   e. _____

6. Notice that footnotes are included in the text where the reference is cited. When preparing the report, include footnotes at the bottoms of the pages on which they are cited. Footnotes also may appear at the end of business reports. Call a corporation in your city or a nearby city and request a copy of their annual report. Review the report to determine how footnotes are placed.

7. Print one copy of the report. Use pagination to number the pages automatically, if supported by your software. Otherwise, number the pages manually.

8. Save the file as EXER27.

Complete the entire exercise before answering the review questions.

Review

1. If you used a pagination function, did you remember to place the page numbers at the top right corner of all pages except page 1? _____

2. Did you enter the footnote numbers as superscripts (numbers that appear raised above the normal line of type)? _____

3. Did you use a block function to underline the subheadings?

_____

Introduction

The "Mail Order" business has become the accepted method for purchasing microcomputers, printers, modems, and related hardware and software during recent years. Although the term "Mail Order" is generally used to describe the ordering of merchandise over the telephone, the items are normally sent by delivery services such as Federal Express or United Parcel Services.

The Right Product

The consumer must be very sure about what is needed. This procedure often translates in to choosing a product from a list of specifications included in an advertisement in a magazine or shoppers' publication. One suggestion is to read reviews that appear in various magazine publications to be sure of ordering a product that has been satisfactory to other consumers or to a research board that reviews the product.[1] {Martin R. Lopez, "Consumers Beware of Mail Order,"PC Review Magazine, April 10, 1991.} Request the name of the salesperson at the mail order business, the exact product specifications, the price, and other pertinent information about the proposed purchase.

Comparison Shopping

Comparison shopping is difficult because it is often hard to be sure that price quotes relate to comparable products. For example, one price quote may be for a PC with a 65 Mb hard drive and a monochrome monitor. Another price quote may be for a similarly equipped PC except one with a 180 Mb hard drive and a Super VGA

Color Monitor. Naturally, the second PC will probably have a higher price, but the extra features may be worth the difference in price.

The name of the sales representative should be recorded. Then, always request that person when inquiring about your order. Request that the sales quote be provided in writing and that the quote include a firm shipping date and component listing. The warranty is also very important. When purchasing a PC, do not purchase one that does not offer a 30-day money back guarantee if you are dissatisfied for any reason.[2] {Betty R. Dunn, "Comparison Shopping," Computer Information Digest, May 24, 1990.} The warranty period is normally for one year. A provision for technical support may also be important when comparison shopping.

Price Quotes

Price quotes should always be in writing, as mentioned above. Ask the sales representative to fax the quote or send it by mail. If you feel that you want a particular dealer's product but have found a better price for a comparable product, do not hesitate to relay this price to permit the dealer to match the price.

Be sure that you know exactly what is included in the price quote. For example, some dealers include the shipping in the sales price while others may add shipping to the price quote. Shipping charges may vary widely—from $30 to $100 for a PC system. Some companies require the purchase of shipping insurance and add this to the cost of the product.

Buyers' Preferences

Customers of mail order businesses are much happier now than a few years ago. Factors of importance to customers are listed below in order of importance:[3] {Randy R. Felker, "Shopping Guide to Mail Orders," PC Catalog, vol. 8, no. 3 (March 1991).} (1) competitive price, (2) quality of the product, (3) product shipped promptly, (4) technical support, (5) wide choice of products, (6) ease of ordering, (7) credit card acceptance, and (8) discounts for volume purchases.

Hidden Charges

Read the advertisement carefully to be sure that all charges are clearly understood. Packing, shipping, and insurance charges are charges that may be clearly defined in the ad. Ask the sales representative for a complete price for a delivered product.

Some dealers offer free on-site repair service for a specific period of time. Others require that the defective equipment be sent to a repair facility. Some dealers offer technical support after the sale. Others charge for this service.

The Purchase

The customer is ready to make the purchase after all details have been considered.

Closing the Deal

Some companies will not accept purchase orders, even from governmental agencies. Some companies wait for 30 days or longer for orders paid for with checks.

Most dealers will accept credit cards such as Visa and MasterCard.

You should indicate clearly the method of payment. Then, determine specifically the dealer's policy for shipping based on your preferred method of payment.

Credit Card Surcharges

Some dealers assess a surcharge for credit card purchases. While there is presently no federal law against these surcharges, some states have state laws that limit or eliminate the surcharge. Both Visa and MasterCard have regulations that prevent a surcharge when these credit cards are used to make a purchase.

Summary

Some mail order dealers may attempt to defraud consumers. However, most computer-related mail order companies must remain honest to maintain a good reputation necessary to stay in business. Most mail order companies provide almost any kind of computer system at a price lower than the retail price. Careful shopping and asking the right questions can help assure a quality product at a reasonable price.

Application 28 **Bibliography**

1. Key a bibliography for the manuscript report completed in Application 27.

2. The three footnotes used in that application are shown on the following page along with an example of bibliographical format. Format the two remaining footnotes for the bibliography.

3. The title "Bibliography" should be centered, in all capital letters, 2 inches from the top of the page and followed by 2 blank lines.

4. Bibliographical entries are single-spaced in alphabetical order, with a double space between each entry. Each line of each entry after the first line is indented five spaces from the left margin.

5. Use a 1.5-inch left margin, a 1-inch right margin, a 2-inch top margin, and a 1-inch bottom margin.

6. Center the page number (6) 1 inch from the bottom of the page.

7. Save the file as EXER28.

8. Print one copy of the bibliography.

> Complete the entire exercise before answering the review questions.

Review

1. What keystroke sequence did you use to indent each line of each entry after the first line? _____

2. Did you place the entries in alphabetical order, according to last name of the author? _____

3. Did you manually center the page numbers, or did you use a page numbering feature? _____

Footnotes to Be Used:

^{1}Martin R. Lopez, "Consumers Beware of Mail Order,"
PC Review Magazine, April 10, 1991.

^{2}Betty R. Dunn, "Comparison Shopping," Computer Information Digest, vol. 5 (May 24, 1990).

^{3}Randy R. Felker, "Shopping Guide to Mail Orders,"
PC Catalog, vol. 8, no. 3 (March 1991).

Bibliographical Format:

Dunn, Betty R. May 24, 1990. Comparison Shopping.
    Computer Information Digest, vol. 5.

Application 29 **Legal Complaint**

1. Key the legal complaint on the following page including the rough draft changes. Indent the paragraphs 10 spaces. Note that money amounts are expressed in both words and figures (with figure amounts placed in parentheses) the first time the amount of money is used. (The amount is expressed in words only after the first time.)

2. Check with a local attorney in your area to obtain copies of complaints and/or other examples of legal documents for exhibiting in your class. Bring the documents to class and share them with the other students. Or, call a legal office and ask about typical forms that are prepared in the office.

3. Refer to a standard dictionary. What is the meaning of the word "Plaintiff"?_____

   What is the meaning of the word "Defendant"?_____

   _____

4. Save the file as EXER29.

5. Print two copies of the legal complaint.

> Complete the entire exercise before answering the review questions.

Review

1. Did you set a tab for the column of parentheses?

   _____

2. Did you double-space the information presented in the caption box? _____

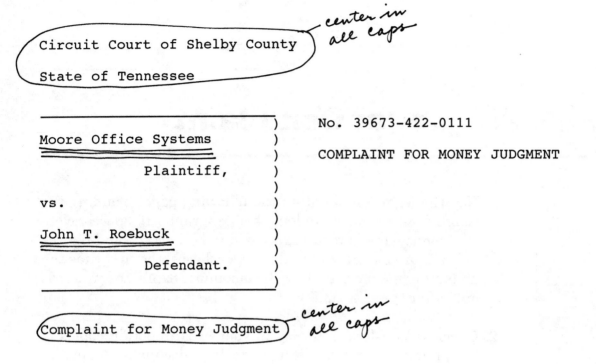

Circuit Court of Shelby County *center in all caps*

State of Tennessee

Moore Office Systems	) No. 39673-422-0111
Plaintiff,	) COMPLAINT FOR MONEY JUDGMENT
vs.	)
John T. Roebuck	)
Defendant.	)

Complaint for Money Judgment *center in all caps*

 COMES NOW the Plaintiff, Moore Office Systems, and commences this proceeding by filing this Complaint for Money Judgment against the Defendant, JOHN T. ROEBUCK, for the sum of ~~Two~~ One Thousand Dollars ($1,000.00), and for cause of action alleges:

 1. Plaintiff is a Tennessee corporation, with principal offices at 2905 Waterleaf Drive, Memphis, Tennessee 38138.

 2. Defendant is a resident of Shelby County residing at 4516 Quince Avenue, Memphis, Tennessee 38117.

 3. That on February 24, 19—, Plaintiff agreed to redecorate the reception area of the main office at 2905 Waterleaf Drive, Memphis, Tennessee, for the sum of Three Thousand Dollars ($3,000.00) by December 31, 19—.

 4. That on February 24, 19—, Plaintiff advanced Defendant the sum of ~~Two~~ One Thousand Dollars ($1,000.00) for supplies and materials.

 5. That Defendant did not complete redecorating work and has not refunded the advance.

6. That Plaintiff has made demand on the Defendant for re-payment of the advance. This payment has not been made by Defendant.

WHEREFORE, Plaintiff prays for a judgment for the full amount of the advance, ~~Two~~ One Thousand Dollars, plus attorney fees and all collection costs.

_____

Rhonda R. Solomito
Attorney for Plaintiff
2905 Waterleaf Drive
Memphis, TN 38138

Application 30 **Form Letter**

1. Retrieve the ASCII file AEXER30 or the WordPerfect file PEXER30 from the Paradigm data disk. Reformat, if necessary. Add codes to permit merging of the inside address and salutation name.

2. Save the form letter as file EXER30P.

3. Prepare a copy of the following inside addresses and salutation names. Add codes to permit the variables to be merged with the prepared form letter.

4. Save the variables as file EXER30S.

5. Print one copy of each of the letters, with variables merged.

> Complete the entire exercise before answering the review questions.

Review

1. What coding did you insert in the form letter to permit variables to be merged? _____

2. How did you code the variables to permit them to be merged into the form letter? _____

Current Date

[Variable 1]

Dear [Variable 2]:

Thank you for accepting our invitation to participate
in a seminar that will include a reception and exhibi-
tion of new software productivity programs.

All meetings will be held at the Holiday Inn North.
The reception will begin at 6:30 P.M., with software
demonstrations to follow at 7 P.M. You should be finished by 8 P.M. Ms. Joan Tillerton, Marketing Representative for your area, will host the reception.

I look forward to your participation in the seminar.
In the meantime, let me know if you need additional information.

Sincerely,

Ronald P. Hightower
Director of Marketing

ri

Enclosure: Seminar Program

<u>Variables</u>

```
---------------------------------------------------------------
Variable 1.  Mr. John A. Milner, President
             Milner and Associates
             712 Ashland Avenue
             Buffalo, NY 14222

Variable 2:  Mr. Milner
---------------------------------------------------------------
Variable 1:  Ms. Betty J. Maniel, President
             Clarkstone Corporation
             65 Niagara Square
             Buffalo, NY 14202

Variable 2:  Ms. Maniel
---------------------------------------------------------------
Variable 1:  Mr. Barry E. Hanson, President
             Derby Corporation of America
             12 Fountain Plaza
             Buffalo, NY 14102

Variable 2:  Mr. Hanson
---------------------------------------------------------------
Variable 1:  Dr. Jay R. Livingston, Director
             Department of Management Information Systems
             State University of New York
             1725 Millersport Highway
             Buffalo, NY 14260

Variable 2:  Dr. Livingston
---------------------------------------------------------------
```

Application 31 **Legal Complaint Template**

1. Retrieve the legal complaint you completed in Application 29. If you did not complete that application, retrieve the ASCII file AEXER31 or the WordPerfect file PEXER31 from the Paradigm data disk.

2. Make the following corrections to the document:

   a. Change the "No." from <u>39673-422-0111</u> to <u>39672-422-0111</u>.

   b. Change the amount <u>One Thousand Dollars ($1,000.00)</u> to <u>One Thousand Two Hundred Fifty Dollars ($1,250.00)</u> each time this particular amount is used in the document.

   c. Change the city <u>Memphis</u> to <u>Germantown</u> each time it is used in the document.

3. Save the corrected document as file EXER31.

4. Print one copy of the corrected legal complaint.

> Complete the entire exercise before answering the review questions.

Review

1. What software feature did you use to find and change all instances of "Memphis" to "Germantown"?

   _____

   _____

2. If you make spelling and/or grammatical errors in a document that becomes part of a legal transaction, what are the possible consequences?

   _____

   _____

   _____

   _____

Application 32 **Form Letter**

1. Retrieve the ASCII file AEXER32 or the WordPerfect file PEXER32 from the Paradigm data disk. Add codes to permit merging of the inside address, salutation name, hotel name, and marketing representative name.

2. Save the form letter as file EXER32P.

3. Key the following inside addresses, salutation names, hotel names, and marketing representative names. Add codes to permit the variables to be merged with the prepared form letter.

4. Save the variables as file EXER32S.

5. Print one copy of each of the letters, with variables merged.

> Complete the entire exercise before answering the review questions.

Review

1. What coding did you include in the form letter to permit merging of the variables? _____

2. How did you code the variables file to permit the inside addresses, salutations, hotel names, and marketing rep names to be merged into the form letter? _____

_____

Current Date

[Variable 1]

Dear [Variable 2]:

Thank you for accepting our invitation to participate
in a seminar that will include a reception and exhibi-
tion of new software productivity programs.

All meetings will be held at the [Variable 3]. The reception will begin at 6:30 P.M., with software demonstrations to follow at 7 P.M. You should be finished
by 8 P.M. [Variable 4], Marketing Representative for
your area, will host the reception.

I look forward to your participation in the seminar.
In the meantime, let me know if you need additional information.

Sincerely,

Ronald P. Hightower
Director of Marketing

ri

Enclosure: Seminar Program

Variables

Variable 1: Dr. Howard H. Lutz, Director
Department of Management Information Systems
University of Akron
302 E. Buchtel Avenue
Akron, OH 44324

Variable 2: Dr. Lutz

Variable 3: Carlton House Hotel

Variable 4: Mr. William R. Boswell

Variable 1: Ms. Hollie R. Heinz, Manager
Heritage Trucking Lines
2121 Windsor Garden Lane
Baltimore, MD 21207

Variable 2: Ms. Heinz

Variable 3: Holiday Inn-Belmont

Variable 4: Mr. Daryl E. Schneider

Variable 1: Mr. Robert A. O'Keefe, President
Mount Pleasant Hospital
3535 Belvedere Avenue
Baltimore, MD 21215

Variable 2: Mr. O'Keefe

Variable 3: Sheraton Inner Harbor

Variable 4: Ms. Chris R. Zeigler

Variable 1: Ms. Angela P. Sholtz, President
Barnwell Sports Centers
15004 Wakki Station
Honolulu, HI 96830

Variable 2: Ms. Sholtz

Variable 3: Hyatt Regency Wakki

Variable 4: Mr. Martin G. Karkera

Application 33 **Customized Letter**

1. Key the seven paragraphs on the next page.

2. Code each paragraph to permit them to be used as form paragraphs (a process called boilerplating). Form paragraphs can be used to customize letters to people who inquire about orders.

3. Save the coded paragraphs as EXER33, or another appropriate name, depending on the software you are using.

4. To create a letter for each person, enter the current date, the inside address, and an appropriate salutation. Then, enter the coding needed to produce the specific paragraphs that will be used with the letter.

5. Print the letter. Repeat the process for the other letters.

> Complete the entire exercise before answering the review questions.

Review

1. Can you think of a salutation that could be used for each letter, thus eliminating the need to key it every time? _____

   _____

2. What other kind of simple, standard response form could you create to respond to customer inquiries? _____

   _____

Form Paragraphs

Paragraph 1

Thank you for your recent order of sporting goods from
our mail order department. Your inquiry about why the
merchandise has not been received has been carefully
reviewed.

Paragraph 2

Your order contained incomplete information relative to
your address. The address has now been corrected. You
should receive the merchandise within 15 days.

Paragraph 3

Your order contained incomplete information relative to
the product number desired. The product number has now
been corrected. You should receive the merchandise
within 15 days.

Paragraph 4

Your order did not include a check to cover the merchandise. Your check has now arrived. Therefore, you
should receive the merchandise within 15 days.

Paragraph 5

The merchandise you requested was temporarily out of
stock in our warehouse. Our stock is now being replen-
ished. You should receive your order within 30 days.

Paragraph 6

I look forward to serving you on future purchases.
Your order will always receive our careful and immedi-
ate attention.

Paragraph 7

Sincerely,

Martin R. Gross, Director
Shipping Department

ri

Mr. John A. Perry
4432 Park Heights Avenue
Baltimore, MD 21215

Paragraphs 1, 3, 6, and 7

Mrs. Billye R. Jenkins
427 W. Kimberly Road
Cedar Rapids, IA 52406

Paragraphs 1, 5, 6, and 7

Dr. Barnard S. North
Seaside Medical Center
1243 Pasadena Avenue
Saint Petersburg, FL 33707

Paragraphs 1, 4, 6, and 7

Prof. George R. Street
Department of Accounting
University of Central Florida
215 Clyde Morris Blvd.
Daytona Beach, FL 32014

Paragraphs 1, 5, 6, and 7

Application 34 **Legal Complaint Template**

1. Retrieve the file EXER29, which you prepared in Application 29. If you did not complete that application, retrieve the ASCII file AEXER34 or the WordPerfect file PEXER34 from the Paradigm data disk.

2. Convert the document to a legal complaint form that will permit the merging of 10 variables into the form. The locations where variables are to be inserted are shown in Example A. Add codes that will permit the merged variables to be inserted into this primary document. For example, the coding needed to merge the first variable will replace the No. 39673-422-0111. The coding needed to merge the second variable will replace the name of the defendant, JOHN T. ROEBUCK. Continue until all coding has been included for each variable in the primary document.

3. Save this revised document as file EXER34P.

4. Key the variables shown in Example B. Add codes to permit the variables to be merged with the prepared legal complaint form.

5. Save this file as EXER34S.

6. Print one copy of each complaint, with the variables merged.

> Complete the entire exercise before answering the review questions.

Review

1. Did you remember to delete punctuation marks, as well as the words in the areas of the original document where variables were to be inserted? _____

2. What other kinds of documents can be turned into customized forms? _____

_____

Example A

CIRCUIT COURT OF SHELBY COUNTY

STATE OF TENNESSEE

)	[Variable 1]
MOORE OFFICE SYSTEMS)	No. ~~39673-422-0111~~
)	
Plaintiff,)	COMPLAINT FOR MONEY JUDGMENT
)	
vs.)	
[Variable 2])	
~~JOHN T. ROEBUCK~~)	
)	
Defendant.)	
)	

COMPLAINT FOR MONEY JUDGMENT

COMES NOW the Plaintiff, Moore Office Systems, and commences this proceeding by filing this Complaint for Money Judgment against the Defendant, [Variable 3] ~~JOHN T. ROEBUCK~~, for the sum of [Variable 4] ~~One Thousand Dollars~~ ~~($1,000.00)~~, and for cause of action alleges:

1. Plaintiff is a Tennessee corporation, with principal offices at 2905 Waterleaf Drive, Memphis, Tennessee 38138.

2. Defendant is a resident of Shelby County residing at [Variable 5] ~~4516 Quince Avenue, Memphis, Tennessee 38117~~.

3. That on [Variable 6] ~~February 24, 19—~~, Plaintiff agreed to redecorate the reception area of the main office at 2905 Waterleaf Drive, Memphis, Tennessee, for the sum of [Variable 7] ~~Three Thousand Dollars ($3,000.00)~~ by December 31, 19—.

4. That on [Variable 8] ~~February 24, 19—~~, Plaintiff advanced Defendant the sum of [Variable 9] ~~One Thousand Dollars~~ for supplies and materials.

5. That Defendant did not complete redecorating work and has not refunded the advance.

6. That Plaintiff has made demand on the Defendant for repayment of the advance. This payment has not been made by Defendant.

WHEREFORE, Plaintiff prays for a judgment for the full
amount of the advance, ~~One Thousand Dollars~~ [*Variable 10*], plus attorney fees and
all collection costs.

_____
Rhonda R. Solomito
Attorney for Plaintiff
2905 Waterleaf Drive
Memphis, TN 38138

Example B

<u>Variables</u>

```
Variable  1:  24856-413-0134
Variable  2:  RALPH R. PHILPOINT
Variable  3:  RALPH R. PHILPOINT
Variable  4:  Two Thousand Dollars ($2,000.00)
Variable  5:  801 White Station Rd., Memphis, Tennessee 38187
Variable  6:  February 19, 19—
Variable  7:  Four Thousand Dollars ($4,000.00)
Variable  8:  February 19, 19—
Variable  9:  Two Thousand Dollars
Variable 10:  Two Thousand Dollars
```

```
Variable  1:  37432-428-0242
Variable  2:  PRENTISS C. SCOTT
Variable  3:  PRENTISS C. SCOTT
Variable  4:  One Thousand Dollars ($1,000.00)
Variable  5:  81 Monroe Avenue, Memphis, Tennessee 38103
Variable  6:  February 15, 19—
Variable  7:  Five Thousand Dollars ($5,000.00)
Variable  8:  February 15, 19—
Variable  9:  One Thousand Dollars
Variable 10:  One Thousand Dollars
```

```
Variable  1:  27345-309-0309
Variable  2:  MARIO R. LOPEZ
Variable  3:  MARIO R. LOPEZ
Variable  4:  One Thousand Five Hundred Dollars ($1,500.00)
Variable  5:  1331 Union Avenue, Memphis, Tennessee 38104
Variable  6:  February 26, 19—
Variable  7:  Four Thousand Dollars ($4,000.00)
Variable  8:  February 26, 19—
Variable  9:  One Thousand Five Hundred Dollars
Variable 10:  One Thousand Five Hundred Dollars
```

Application 35 **Letter Template**

---

1. Retrieve the file EXER33 you completed in Application 33.

2. Use the form paragraphs to create customized letters for the following three persons. Print a copy of each letter.

Letter Addresses

```
Ms. Margaret A. Johnson
4420 W. Markham
Little Rock, AR   72202

Paragraphs 1, 2, 6, and 7
-----------------------------------------------------
Mr. Thomas P. Burns, Jr.
3206 Landover Street
Alexandria, VA 22305

Paragraphs 1, 4, 6, and 7
-----------------------------------------------------
Prof. James T. Taylor
Department of Management
Weber State University
3750 Harrison Road
Ogden, UT 84406

Paragraphs 1, 3, 6, and 7
-----------------------------------------------------
```

Review

1. Did you retrieve and view the form paragraphs before inserting them in the letter? _____

2. Is it necessary to proofread each letter before you send it out? Why or why not? _____

Application 36 **Form Letter Template**

1. Retrieve the file EXER30S you completed in Application 30.

2. Delete Betty J. Maniel from the mailing list.

3. Add the following names listed to the mailing list.

4. Save the updated mailing list as file EXER36S.

5. Key form letters for the five names on the updated mailing list using the file EXER30P as the primary file.

> Complete the entire exercise before answering the review questions.

Review

1. Why is it necessary to update a mailing list?_____
   _____
   _____
   _____

2. Did you remember to include the necessary coding for the names that are to be added to the mailing list? _____
   _____

Variables

```
-----------------------------------------------------------
Variable 1:  Dr. Stanley R. Smith, M.D.
             Sheehan Memorial Hospital
             435 Michigan Avenue
             Buffalo, NY 14203

Variable 2:  Dr. Smith
-----------------------------------------------------------
Variable 1:  Ms. Kathy J. Kennedy, President
             Kennedy, Kennedy, and Jones Attorneys
             111 West Huron
             Buffalo, NY 14202

Variable 2:  Ms. Kennedy
-----------------------------------------------------------
```

Name _____

Section _____ Date _____

Application 37 **Manuscript Template**

1. Retrieve the file EXER27 you completed in Application 27.

2. Make the following revisions to the manuscript.

3. Save the revised manuscript as file EXER37.

4. Print one copy of the revised manuscript.

Hint

Page number changes (or repagination) may be required. Also note that some adjustment of footnotes may be required to assure that they appear on pages where they are cited.

Hint

When searching for and replacing words, do not replace words in proper names such as magazine titles.

<u>Revisions to Manuscript</u>

1. Add the following paragraph at the end of "The Purchase" section: All factors should be considered prior to making the purchase. Be sure that all details relative to the purchase are well understood by all parties and that all terms and conditions are stated in writing.

2. Add the following sentence at the end of the last paragraph in the "Credit Card Surcharges" section: The surcharge, if any, is normally 5 percent of the purchase price.

3. Use the search and replace option, if available with your software, to replace "PC" with "microcomputer" each time it is used in the manuscript. Note: If this option is not available, review the manuscript and make the changes manually. Make revisions for capital letters as needed after the replacement is completed.

4. Add a paragraph at the end of the "Summary" section that includes price quotes and information about comparison shopping. What wording do you consider appropriate?

_____

_____

_____

_____

Application 38 Unit Mastery

Word processing applications often require that two or more files be used when preparing a final document. Previously, you have completed a title page, table of contents, manuscript, footnotes, and bibliography for parts of a report involving mail order sales. George R. Scott, Director of Mail Order Sales, needs the complete report to answer a request from a customer who is considering ordering microcomputer products through the mail.

Mr. Scott needs the final, completed report so that it can be sent to the prospective customer, Mr. George McCullough. A letter of transmittal to accompany the report is also needed.

1. This application requires the following files: EXER25, from Application 25; EXER26, from Application 26; EXER27, from Application 27; and EXER28, from Application 28. Retrieve and review on your monitor each of the documents in these files.

2. Move each footnote to a new page at the end of the manuscript. Center the word "footnotes" in all capital letters 2 inches from the top of the page, followed by two blank lines. Then, enter each of the footnotes in the same order and format as in the original manuscript. Note: Reformat the pages as needed (if not done automatically by the software program).

3. Write (key) a one-paragraph summary of the report's recommendations. Title it Abstract, and print one copy to be included with the letter of transmittal.

4. Number the pages in consecutive order as follows: Title Page (i)—but do not print the number, Table of Contents (ii), Manuscript (1-4), Footnotes (5), and Bibliography (6). Page numbers should appear centered, 1 inch from the bottom on these pages: Table of Contents, first page of the Manuscript, Footnotes, and Bibliography. Otherwise, page numbers should appear in the upper right corner.

5. Redesign the Title Page using a different font or other design features available with your software. Reprint this page.

6. Print one copy of the complete report, including the Title Page, Table of Contents, Manuscript, Footnotes, and Bibliography. Save the report, if desired.

7. Key the letter on page 116, incorporating the rough draft changes. Use right-margin justification for the body. Print one copy. Your final project should include the letter of transmittal, the abstract, and the complete report.

Hint

Note that a number is not printed on the title page but that it is considered page 1.

Hint

Business reports often contain a brief summary, or "abstract," of the report's conclusions.

Current Date

Mr. George McCullough
2553 S. Alameda
Corpus Cristi, TX 78411

Dear Mr. McCullough:

The report that you requested about ^mail ordering microcomputer products ~~by mail order~~ is attached.

Mail order is a fast and efficient way to ^purchase ~~order~~ products. ~~However,~~ be sure that you comparison shop, obtain price quotes in writing from several sources, and check for hidden charges prior to placing an order through the mail. The report ^will ~~should~~ provide you with additional information.

Thank you for your interest in mail order shopping. Our mail order department is ready to serve your microcomputer needs. We are just a phone call away. (1-800-555-2783)

Sincerely,

George R. Scott, Director
Mail Order Sales Department

ri

Attachment: *Report on Mail Ordering*

Unit 4

Special Features

This unit includes a variety of word processing applications. The use of mathematical functions such as adding single and multiple columns of figures is presented in Applications 39 and 40. An organizational chart in Application 41 provides an opportunity to use the line draw feature. Application 42 offers the opportunity to use a graphic in text material.

In Application 43 you will import a spreadsheet document into a letter. Applications 44 and 45 provide practice in revising a budget and the organizational chart created earlier.

The unit simulation, Application 46, provides a format for completing a form document containing a graphic feature. Application 47, called "Workplace Challenge," is the final exercise in this book. This application simulates a project you might encounter in an office setting and requires you to apply some advanced word processing skills and features.

Application 39 **Budget**

1. Key the budget on the following page. Incorporate all the rough draft changes. Enter the expense amounts in a tab format that will permit them to be totaled.

2. Notice that the total has not been computed. Use the math function, if available with your software, to compute the total. Otherwise, use an electronic calculator or compute the total by hand.

3. Save the file as EXER39.

4. Print one copy of the budget.

5. Using these same procedures, key a personal budget that you feel is appropriate for you for next month. Print one copy of your monthly budget. Discuss this budget with a friend to determine whether or not it is reasonable.

> Complete the entire exercise before answering the review questions.

Review

1. Did you align the digits? _____

2. What feature or keystrokes did you use to make the total appear directly underneath the amounts? _____

_____

center over budget

(Personal Budget
for Dave Davidson
Month of June, 19—)

Expenses   Amounts

Rent   875
Utilities   225
Food   580
Clothing   ~~85~~ 125
Car expenses   ~~178~~ 218
Car payment   350
Medical   ~~57~~ 117
Entertainment   176
Insurance   150
Credit card   ~~185~~ 207
Savings   ~~290~~ 250
Miscellaneous   100

        Total

Application 40 **Trial Balance**

---

1. Key the trial balance on the following page. Incorporate all rough draft changes. Enter the trial balance amounts in a tab format that will permit them to be totaled.

2. Notice that the total for each column has not been computed. Use the math function, if available with your software, to compute the totals. Otherwise, use an electronic calculator or compute the totals by hand.

3. Save the file as EXER40.

4. Print two copies of the trial balance.

> Complete the entire exercise before answering the review questions.

Review

1. Did you align the digits in each column? _____

2. The Debits and Credits must equal each other. Do your totals match? _____

center over trial balance

Trial Balance
Corner Market
December 31, 19—

Account	Debit	Credit
Cash	$10,000	
Accounts Receivable	4,000	
Store Supplies	~~500~~ 575	
Office Supplies	~~300~~ 325	
Prepaid Insurance	~~700~~ 825	
Equipment	5,000	
Accounts Payable		$ ~~500~~ 725
N. M. Grand, Capital		16,900
Sales		5,600
Salary Expense	1,350	
Rent Expense	1,150	
Total		

Application 41 **Organization Chart**

1. Prepare an organization chart, using the information on the following page.

2. Draw lines to form rectangles around the corporate titles. Some software packages have line draw features to permit drawing the lines and other packages permit drawing rectangles. If your software does not have these features, you may use a black ink pen.

3. Think about the organizational structure used at the school you attend. How is the structure shown here similar to or different from the one used at your school? _____

   _____

4. Save the file as EXER41.

5. Print one copy of the organization chart.

> Complete the entire exercise before answering the review questions.

Review

1. Do your lines form rectangles around the position titles?

   _____

2. Did you use lines to connect the various positions?

   _____

BROOKSON INNS ORGANIZATION CHART

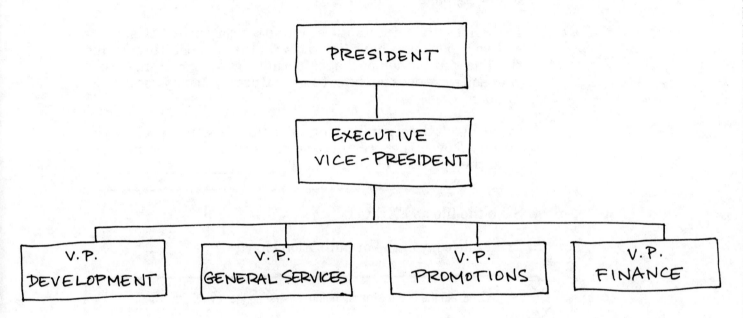

Application 42 **Flyer**

---

1. Create the following flyer. Include graphics similar to the ones shown in the flyer. Try to place the graphics in the locations shown. Adjust the size of the images as appropriate. If your software program does not permit graphics, leave spaces for the images. Then cut out the pictures and paste them onto your keyed document.

2. Text in the flyer should be printed with right margin justification.

3. Save the file as EXER42.

4. Print one copy of the flyer.

> Complete the entire exercise before answering the review questions.

Review

1. Did you prepare the text portion of the flyer first?_____

2. Does the text flow around the graphics? _____

3. Did you need to change the size of the graphics to make them compatible with the size of the flyer?_____

NEW PRODUCT ANNOUNCEMENT

Electronic Products International is proud to announce a new product line that will save you much money as you begin to consider purchases of microcomputer products for this year. The date is just around the corner. Mark your calendar for big savings.

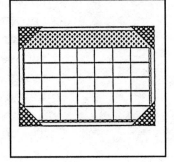

Feel free to call our courteous sales staff to discuss products or to determine the right product line to meet your needs. Someone will be happy to talk with you on the telephone or meet with you in your office.

Your time is important, so you will want to do business with a company that has adequate resources to handle your most difficult problems and answer your technical questions. Service after the sale is an important part of our philosophy for serving the needs of our customers.

Please visit our office showroom at 2343 Kimbrook Boulevard or call 555-2734 for a private meeting in our display center or your office.

Application 43 **Table**

1. Key the following letter, with the table included.

2. If you are using the Paradigm data disk, retrieve the file AEXER43.PRN (or PEXER43.PRN if you are using WordPerfect). Note: This file has been created using Lotus® 1-2-3® and saved as an ASCII file. If you are <u>not</u> using the Paradigm data disk or your software program does <u>not</u> permit importing the file, you will have to key the table into the letter.

3. Save the file as EXER43.

4. Print one copy of the letter.

> Complete the entire exercise before answering the review questions.

Review

1. What coding did you use to import the spreadsheet (Lotus 1-2-3) file into your word processing document? _____

   _____

2. Did you need to adjust the location of the spreadsheet table in the letter to improve the letter's appearance? _____

   _____

Current Date

Mr. George A. DeFlore
376 Biscayne Boulevard Way
Miami, FL   33131

Dear Mr. DeFlore:

Thank you for requesting information about a typical
mortgage payment schedule in the $15,000 to $55,000
range. A schedule copy is shown below.

        <Note: Import or insert payment schedule here.>

If you have questions or need additional information,
please let me know.

Sincerely,

Rebecca Humber
Finance Manager

ri

A1: [W10]   READY

	A	B	C	D	E	F
1		FINANCIAL AMERICAN MORTGAGE COMPANY				
2		PAYMENT SCHEDULE				
3	------	------	------	------	------	------
4	Mortgage	Length of	Interest	Monthly	Total	
5	Amount	Loan (Years)	Rate	Pr. & Int.	Payments	
6	------	------	------	------	------	------
7	$15,000	15	12.00%	$183.53	$33,035.45	
8	$16,000	15	12.00%	$195.77	$35,237.82	
9	$17,000	15	11.75%	$205.23	$36,941.67	
10	$18,000	15	11.75%	$217.30	$39,114.70	
11	$19,000	15	11.50%	$226.30	$40,733.44	
12	$20,000	20	11.50%	$216.17	$51,881.91	
13	$25,000	20	11.50%	$270.22	$64,852.39	
14	$30,000	20	11.50%	$324.26	$77,822.87	
15	$35,000	30	11.00%	$335.49	$120,775.83	
16	$40,000	30	11.00%	$383.42	$138,029.52	
17	$45,000	30	10.75%	$422.89	$152,240.72	
18	$50,000	30	10.75%	$469.88	$169,156.35	
19	$55,000	30	10.50%	$506.59	$182,371.99	
20	------	------	------	------	------	------

11-Nov-90   04:14 PM

Table • 129

Application 44 **Budget Template**

1. Retrieve the file EXER39, which you created in Application 39. If you did not complete Application 39, retrieve the ASCII file AEXER44 or the WordPerfect file PEXER44 from the Paradigm data disk.

2. Make the following changes to the budget.

3. Save the revised budget as file EXER44.

4. Print two copies of the budget.

Complete the entire exercise before answering the review questions.

Review

1. When you retrieved the original budget from the disk, did you review the structure of the budget, including coding needed to permit math computations? _____

2. Did you check the total to insure that an appropriate computation was completed? _____

PERSONAL BUDGET
for Dave Davidson
Month of June, 19—

Expenses	Amounts
Rent	~~875~~ 885
Utilities	225
Food	580
Clothing	~~125~~ 150
Car expenses	218
Car payment	350
Medical	117
Entertainment	176
Insurance	~~150~~ 175
Credit card	207
Savings	250
Miscellaneous	100
Total	3,373

note: Total should reflect changed amounts.

Application 45 **Organization Chart**

Hint

Do not use a proportional spacing font when using a line draw feature.

1. Retrieve the file EXER41, which you created in Application 41. If you did not complete Application 41, retrieve the ASCII file AEXER45 or the WordPerfect file PEXER45 from the Paradigm data disk.

2. Make the changes to the following organization chart.

3. Save the revised organization chart as file EXER45.

4. Print two copies of the organization chart.

Complete the entire exercise before answering the review questions.

Hint

Draw all lines first. Then erase lines that are not needed or lines that were made in error.

Review

1. Did you key the text first? _____

2. Did you use the line draw feature, if available with your software program, to draw the lines in the organizational chart? _____

BROOKSON INNS ORGANIZATION CHART

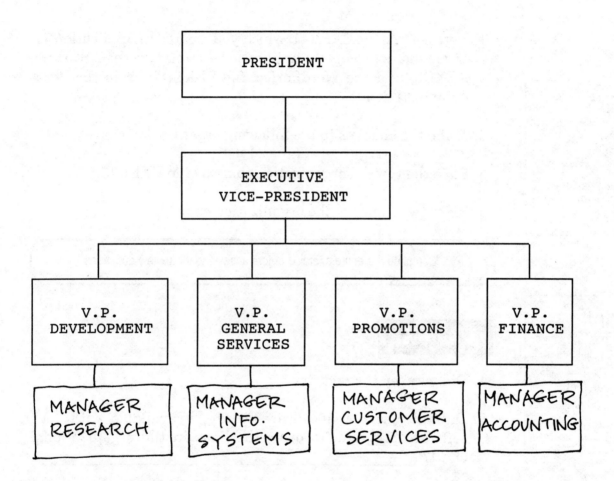

Application 46 **Simulation**

You work in the Graphic Arts Department of a stationery company. Several client companies have requested information about an appropriate design to use for letterheads in their legal departments.

Mr. Martin, your supervisor, has designed a graphic that he considers appropriate for use in legal departments. He has asked you to prepare a letter containing the design of a gavel. You are to send this letter as a response to the requests for a legal letterhead design.

1. Key the form letter shown in Example A so that it can be sent to each of the four persons listed in Example B. (You also used this list in Application 30.)

2. Use a mail merge feature to prepare the letters.

3. The symbol included in the letter should be similar to the one used in Example A. In the event that your software does not support graphics, leave a space for the graphic design.

4. Draw a line around the graphic.

5. Save the form letter as file EXER46.

6. Print a copy of the form letter to each of the persons on the mailing list.

Example A

<u>Form Letter</u>

Date

[Variable 1]

Dear [Variable 2]:

Thank you for requesting that our company supply
you with an appropriate graphic design for the
letterhead of your company's legal department.
The design that our Graphics Arts Department has
chosen for your review is shown below.

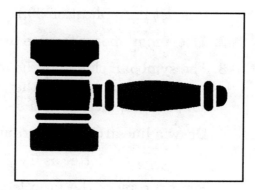

While designing the symbol, we followed your
suggestion to use a very simple design that
signifies the legal profession. I look forward
to your evaluation and suggestions after reviewing
the design.

Sincerely,

Martin E. Calloway, Artist
Graphics Arts Department

ri

Example B

```
-----------------------------------------------------------------
Variable 1:  Mr. John A. Milner, President
             Milner and Associates
             712 Ashland Avenue
             Buffalo, NY  14222

Variable 2:  Mr. Milner
-----------------------------------------------------------------
Variable 1:  Ms. Betty J. Maniel, President
             Clarkstone Corporation
             65 Niagara Square
             Buffalo, NY  14202

Variable 2:  Ms. Maniel
-----------------------------------------------------------------
Variable 1:  Mr. Barry E. Hanson, President
             Derby Corporation of America
             12 Fountain Plaza
             Buffalo, NY  14102

Variable 2:  Mr. Hanson
-----------------------------------------------------------------
Variable 1:  Dr. Jay R. Livingston, Director
             Department of Management Information Systems
             State University of New York
             1725 Millersport Highway
             Buffalo, NY  14260

Variable 2:  Dr. Livingston
-----------------------------------------------------------------
```

Application 47 **Workplace Challenge**

TO: Administrative Assistant

FROM: Nancy Boyd, Marketing Director

DATE: Current Date

SUBJECT: Report Development

The office in Los Angeles requested my attendance at a sales conference on Monday. Therefore, I came to the office today (Saturday) to prepare materials for the conference. I was able to locate the needed materials with only a few exceptions. I need you to prepare the three documents shown below as quickly as possible on Monday morning and fax them to me in Los Angeles. The fax number is 800-555-7823.

Where appropriate, I have made notations on the materials to let you know what is needed. I appreciate your willingness to complete these materials for me on short notice. I will be back in the office on Wednesday.

Document 1

Prepare the table shown below, except please make the text and figures in the table larger so that they can be converted to a transparency for my sales presentation. Center the table on the page so that it looks good. I think your word processing program has a math function that you can use to compute the total.

QUARTERLY SALES FIGURES[1]

Quarter 1	238,490
Quarter 2	254,389
Quarter 3	232,673
Quarter 4	263,409

Total

[1]Source: Annual Sales Report

Note: Please show as a superscript.

Document 2

Use the line draw feature to box the sales figures for each quarter. Follow the format shown below. This report will also be used for my sales presentation, but use normal size fonts.

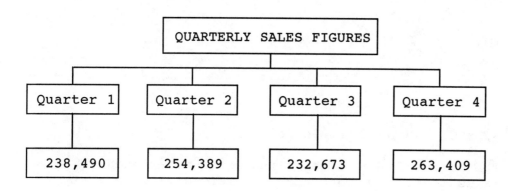

Document 3

Compose a short (one paragraph) description of the sales trends for the four quarters. Use "Sales Trends and Figures" as the main title. Use two columns for the report. Include your description in one column on the page. Include the above sales numbers as a boxed figure in a second column on the page. You may have to include the first quarter under the table heading (QUARTERLY SALES FIGURES), the second quarter under the first quarter, the third quarter under the second quarter, and so forth to make it fit into the column. I would like for each of the figures to be boldfaced.

Proofreaders' Marks

Desired Change/ Proofreaders' Mark	Example	Revised Copy
Transpose ⌐⌐ or ∽	Run the |program |computer|.	Run the computer program.
	or	or
	Second, turn on the CPU. First, insert the disk.	First, insert the disk. Second, turn on the CPU.
Insert ∧ ∨	*strike* Turn the monitor and ∨ENTER. ∧ *on*	Turn on the monitor and strike ENTER.
Close up space ⌒	Typ⌒ing is fun.	Typing is fun.
Add space # /	Quality work is a#priority.	Quality work is a priority.
Delete ♂ or ✗	Computers are (very) dependable.	Computers are dependable.
	or	or
	Some computers have disks.	Some computers have disks.
Lowercase *lc* or /	*lc* Every Programmer is accurate.	Every programmer is accurate.
	or	or
	Learning Machine language is difficult.	Learning machine language is difficult.
Uppercase *uc* or ≡	*uc* come to the computer display.	Come to the computer display.
	or	or
	come to the software show. ≡	Come to the software show.
Move left ⊏	⊏ Planning your work is fun.	Planning your work is fun.
Move right ⊐	Unpl⊐anned work is chaotic.	Unplanned work is chaotic.

Desired Change/ Proofreaders' Mark	Example	Revised Copy
Single-space *ss*	Make more income. *ss* Try hard and succeed.	Make more income. Try hard and succeed.
Double-space *ds*	The lazy usually fail. Turn off the computer. *ds*	The lazy usually fail. Turn off the computer.
Triple-space *ts*	Turn off the color monitor. *ts* You are learning very fast.	Turn off the color monitor. You are learning very fast.
Move as shown	The computer (basic) system	The basic computer system
Let stand *stet*	*stet* Three (major) components	Three major components
Spell out ○ *sp*	*sp* The (U.S.) is a great place to live.	The United States is a great place to live.
New paragraph ¶	¶It is best if you learn proofreaders' marks.	It is best if you learn proofreaders' marks.
Underline _____	The title was, <u>How to</u> <u>Keyboard More Effectively.</u>	The title was, <u>How to</u> <u>Keyboard More Effectively</u>
Run in	Long-range planning is necessary for effective planning.	Long-range planning is necessary for effective planning.

Appendix

Tutorial for Word Processing Using WordPerfect 5.0 (or above)

This tutorial assists the learning process when using this book and the WordPerfect software program. Instructions assume that you have a basic knowledge of WordPerfect and have accessed the WordPerfect screen.

All commands to be entered in this tutorial appear in boldface, for example, **F10, A:PEXER18, Enter.** These instructions indicate that you should press the F10 key, enter A:PEXER18 and then press the Enter key. The A: part of the entry will cause the document to be stored on drive A. Check with your instructor to determine the drive designation where you will store data files. Examples in this text use the drive A designation, but you will use the one that relates to your microcomputer configuration.

When two keys are required to perform a function, a + will be used. For example, **Alt + F1** indicates that the user should press the Alternate key, the F1 key, and then release both keys at the same time.

Read the instructions in the book carefully for each application. Instructions in this tutorial will then indicate specific keys and entries to produce the desired results. Instructions included in one application will normally not be repeated if the same function is needed in a later application. Remember how to perform the function from previous experiences or review the tutorial for the previous application.

Some applications contain instructions to retrieve one of two files, depending on whether or not you use the Paradigm data disk.

A word of caution: You will be provided with commands throughout the tutorial to aid in completion of the applications. If you just push the buttons, limited learning will occur. If you watch the screen and study the commands as you enter them, you will learn how to complete the functions quickly.

Application 1: Letter

- Enter the letter as shown with all rough draft changes.

- To use the thesaurus, first move the cursor to the beginning of the word "complete" in the letter. Press **Alt + F1**. Review the screen to determine if an appropriate word exists. If so, press **1** and then press the letter that corresponds to the appropriate word. The word in the letter should now be replaced.

- To save the completed document, press **F7, Yes, A:EXER1, Enter**. The document should now be saved to drive A. Enter **No** to remain in WordPerfect or **Yes** to leave WordPerfect.

- To retrieve a document, press **F5 A: Enter**. Highlight the desired filename from the directory menu and then enter **1** to retrieve the document. Note other options on the menu to perform other operations with the highlighted file.

- To add text, simply move to the place in the document where text is to be added and do so. Note: Pressing **Ins** will toggle from insert to typeover. Try this a few times, but remain in the insert mode while typing a document to avoid deleting text accidentally.

- To boldface existing text, move the cursor to the first character of the text to be boldfaced, press **Alt + F4** to switch to the block mode, press the **arrow key** until the text is highlighted, and then press **F6**.

- You may want to press Reveal Codes to see that the boldface code has been added to the text. To access Reveal Codes, press **Alt + F3 or F11**, if available on your keyboard. To leave Reveal Codes, repeat this process.

- To print a document that you have on the screen, press **Shift + F7, 1** to print multiple pages or **2** to print only one page of the document. Review the print menu to see other print options available.

- The save, retrieve, and print functions are used in most applications. The steps needed for these functions will not be repeated in the tutorial.

Application 2: Memorandum

- To center the first line of text, press **Shift + F6**, then key the text to be centered, and press **Enter**.

- To underline text, press **F8**, key the text to be underlined, and press **F8** again.

- To underline existing text, move the cursor to the first character of text to be underlined, press **Alt + F4** to switch to the block mode, press the **arrow key** until the text appears highlighted, then press **F8**.

- Set a tab stop at the place where the parts of the memorandum heading begin. To do this press **Shift + F8, 1, 8, Ctrl + End** Then move the cursor to the point on the format line where the tab should be set and enter **L**. Press **F7** twice to return to the document.

- Delete letters and words by moving the cursor to the point where the letters begin and press **Del** until the characters are deleted from the screen. To delete a block of text such as a sentence or paragraph, move the cursor to the beginning of the text as done previously. Then press **Alt + F4** for the block mode, highlight the text to be deleted, and then press **Del Yes**. Note: The cursor can be moved during highlighting by pressing the arrow key or by pressing a character that appears later in the text. For example, pressing . (period) will highlight the entire sentence.

Application 3: Letter

- Move the cursor to the beginning of the word *Colorodo* to check spelling of the word. Press **Ctrl + F2 1** (to check at word level), **A** (to choose the correct spelling), **F7** (to exit the spellchecking function).

- Review the tutorial for the previous application for an example of block deleting.

- Move the cursor to the beginning of the text to be copied. Press **Alt + F4**, highlight the text to be copied, press **Ctrl + F4, 1, 2**, move the cursor to the place where the text will be copied to, and press **Enter**. The text should now be copied from the original location to the new location in the document.

- To move the paragraph, move the cursor to the first character in the paragraph to be moved, press **Ctrl + F4, 2** to highlight the text to be moved, press **1**, then move the cursor to the place where the text will be moved to and press **Enter**.

- To add lines, move to the beginning of the line where a blank line is to be added and press **Enter**. Likewise, move to the beginning of blank lines to be deleted and press **Del**.

- As always, be sure to note other options on the various menus as you complete functions. This is critical to learning to perform the functions instead of merely pushing keys.

Application 4: Customer List

- Move the cursor to the beginning of the line to be centered horizontally and press **Shift + F6** prior to keying the text to be centered. Pressing **Enter** exits the centering function.

- Prior to the section of lines that are to be placed flush with the right margin, press **Shift + F8, 1, 3, 3**, and **F7**. After keying the three lines, shift back to left-margin justification by repeating the preceding steps, except that *left* will be chosen on the appropriate menu instead of *right*. You can also use **Alt-F6** to place text flush with the right margin.

- Set appropriate tabs to permit indentions for each of the 10 entries on the customer list. See Application 2 to review setting of tabs if needed.

- Arrangement of the names in alphabetical order will require a rekeying of the address list or blocking and moving each address.

- Notice that you will be asked whether or not you want to replace the document as you save the revised document. Enter **Yes**. The revised document will now replace the original document on the disk.

Application 5: Newsletter

- To change the margins, press **Shift + F8, 7, 2, Enter, 2, Enter**. Press **F7** to return to the document.

- Enter the main heading, horizontally centered and underlined. To underline text press **F8**, key the text, and press **F8**.

- Move the cursor to the beginning of the text to be used for spellchecking. Press **Ctrl + F2** and press **1, 2,** or **3** depending on how much of the document is to be spellchecked.

- To change to automatic hyphenation, press **Shift + F8, 1, 2, Y** (Yes). Press **F7** to return to the document.

Application 6: Letter

- Use WordPerfect's default tab of 5 spaces to indent the paragraphs.

- Format again to set tabs for the table included in the letter. Note that you do not normally set tabs for column headings. After the table has been keyed, format again for a 5-space paragraph indention.

- Although tab setting in this exercise is on a more difficult level than previously, prior instructions for setting tabs should suffice for this application.

- To adjust to new margins, press **Shift + F8, 1, 7, 1.5, Enter, 1.5, Enter, F7**

Application 7: Sales Invoice

- WordPerfect supports the line draw function for drawing lines. The best approach is to enter all text in the document prior to drawing the horizontal and vertical lines.

- Line draw permits you to use the four arrow keys to draw lines with the cursor. Position the cursor where you want the drawing to begin. Press **Ctrl + F3, 2, 1**, and use the appropriate arrow key to make the first line. After the line has been made, press **6** and move the cursor to the point where the second line is to be drawn. Press **1** and use the appropriate arrow to draw the second line. Use the above procedure until all lines have been drawn. Press **F7** to exit from line draw.

- As you experiment with line draw, you will probably draw lines in places where they are not needed. It is better to draw all lines and then erase at the end as needed. Simply choose **5** and use the arrow to move along the line to be erased. Pressing **1** again will move back into line draw. You may want to practice drawing lines, erasing lines, and moving prior to beginning the document.

Application 8: Customer List Template

- Use tabs to create two columns. Divide your address list in half first so you know which address will be at the top of column two. WordPerfect also has a columns feature, which will be introduced in Application 15.

Application 9: Letter Template

- The functions included in this application were introduced previously. However, this application requires extensive text editing and insertion of an itemized listing. The document should be formatted to permit tabs for the itemized listing.

Application 10: Sales Invoice Template

- Retrieve the sales invoice form created in Application 7.

- Appropriate tab settings should be made. Notice that you should enter **D** on the format line to set decimal tabs.

- Press **Ins** to toggle to typeover mode as you enter information on the sales invoice.
- Exit this document after completion and printing. Retrieve the sales invoice form and complete the second invoice.

Application 11: Simulation

- This application includes many of the functions and features presented in applications 1 to 10. However, no new functions are included in this application.

Application 12: Passenger List

- WordPerfect's search feature permits the scanning of a document to find designated text or codes.
- Move the cursor to the beginning of the text to be searched. Press **F2** to obtain the *Srch:* prompt. Enter the text to be located — ***Blanche W. Carter*** in the first instance. Press **F2** to begin the search. The cursor should stop when the name is located in the document.
- Repeat these steps for each name to be located.
- To replace *311* with *375*, move the cursor to the beginning of the text to be searched and press **Alt + F2, N, 311, F2, 375, F2**

Application 13: Invitation

- Press **Ctrl + F8** and **4** to obtain a listing of the base fonts available with your software program. Highlight the desired font and press **1** to select the font and return to the document.
- To change the size of the font, press **Ctrl + F8** and **1** to access the size menu. Press a number to choose a size and return to the document.
- The selected font and size will remain in effect until changed. To return to the default font, press **Ctrl + F8, 3.**

Application 14: Help Wanted Ad

- Use the font change steps introduced in application 13 while completing this application.

Application 15: Journal Advertisement

- Dividing the ad into columns requires four steps: defining the columns, turning on the column mode, keying the text material, and turning off the column mode.
- Position the cursor at the location where you want to begin the column format. To define the columns press **Alt + F7, 1, 3,** make changes to the text column definition menu screen if desired, and press **F7** twice. To turn on column mode press **Alt + F7, 1,** and **1.** Enter the text. To turn off column mode press **Alt + F7, 1, and 2.**
- After the left column is full, text will begin in the second column automatically. Notice that there is more text in the left column than in the right column. To distribute the text evenly, move the cursor to the beginning of the appropriate line (halfway point) and press **Enter** until the text is moved to the right column. Delete blank lines in the right column as needed to join the text.

- To move the cursor from the right column to the left column, press **Ctrl + Home** and then the **left arrow key**. To move from the left column to the right column, press **Ctrl + Home** and then the **right arrow key**. This movement between columns is necessary if editing is required.

- You can use the compose feature to create typeset-quality bullet characters. To create bullets, press **Ctrl + V** to access the *Key =* prompt. Enter * (asterisk) and then one of the following characters:

  . (period) for a small, filled bullet

  * (asterisk) for a medium, filled bullet

  o (lowercase o) for a small, hollow bullet

  O (uppercase O) for a large, hollow bullet

Application 16:   Report

- Change the line spacing format several times to achieve the indicated spacing. Many style manuals now permit double-spacing before and after side headings, but triple-spacing was required here to provide extra practice with changing spacing formats.

- To enter the superscript, press **Ctrl + F8, 1** to select size and **1** to select superscript. Then type the footnote number in the text document. Then change back to normal size by pressing **Ctrl + F8** and **3**. If your printer has half-line capabilities, the footnote number will print as a smaller number when you use footnote commands (**Ctrl-F7**).

- To use footnote commands, press **Ctrl + F7, 1, 1.** Key the footnote text and press **F7**. The footnote will not appear on the monitor but will appear on the printed page.

Application 17:   Outline

- To create the header, press **Shift + F8, 2, 3, 1, 2,** key **Return to Room 1411** and press **F7** twice.

- Press **Ctrl + Enter** to create a hard page break. Note that a double line (======) appears across the document to indicate a hard page break.

- If it becomes necessary to delete a hard page break, press **Alt + F3** or **F11** to access Reveal Codes. Delete the coding ([HPg]) and press **Alt + F3** or **F11** to exit Reveal Codes.

- The end of a natural page (soft page break) will be indicated by a single line (-------------) across the document.

Application 18:   Letter

- Use **Ctrl-F2** to access the spellchecker. When a word is located that is not in the dictionary, it will be highlighted with available options listed across the bottom of the screen. The screen will often contain words that are found in the dictionary that are similar to the one in your document. In these instances, you can enter the letter that corresponds to the correct word if it is in the list. At the end of the spellcheck, press any key to return to the document.

- The thesaurus can be accessed by pressing **Alt + F1**. A list of words that can possibly be used in place of the word in your document appears on the screen. Enter a letter to select one of the words to replace the word in the document. Then enter **1** to replace the word.

Application 19: Letterhead

- Choices of fonts and font sizes were discussed previously. This application provides practice with document layout. Experiment with several layouts until one is developed that is appropriate for the application.

- To view the names of graphic files available for use, press **F5**, enter the disk drive designation, such as **A:** or **C:**, and look for files with the extension *.wpg*. Any file appearing with this extension is a graphic file. Press **F7** to return to the document.

- To import the graphic, place the cursor at the point where the graphic will appear on the letterhead and press **Alt + F9**, **1** for figure, **4** for options, and make desired entries from the 9 options available. Then, press **Alt + F9** again, **1** for figure, **1** to create, **1** for filename prompt, key the name of the graphic to be imported including the extension *.wpg*, and press **Enter**. (Notice that you can change the size of the figure box and other definitions at this time, if desired.) Press **F7** to return to the document. The graphic should now appear in your document. Press **Shift + F7** and **6** to view the document with the graphic.

Application 20: Table

- Decide on appropriate tab settings for the table. Note that the third column includes decimal values.

- Press **Shift + F8, 1**, and **8** to access the format line. Press **Ctrl + End** to erase all tab settings. Move to the place on the line where the first tab is to be set and press **L** to set a left tab. Move to the place on the line where the decimal point will appear and press **D** to set a decimal tab. Press **F7** twice to return to the document.

- The usual practice is not to use tabs while entering column headings. They are normally entered with estimated spaces between each one. After the table is completed, move the cursor between the column headings and press **Space Bar** or **Del** to add or delete spaces between the headings.

Application 21: Passenger List Template

- Revisions to the passenger list created in Application 12 will be made for this application.

- Delete information from each line that will not be needed after column headings are added.

- Change the format to include appropriate tab settings for the second and third columns. Press **Tab** on each line at the point where a tab is required.

- Suggested column headings: Name, Flight, and Departure.

Application 22: Report Template

- Move the cursor to the beginning of the document. Press **Shift + F8, 1**, and **7** to access the margin selection menu. Enter the appropriate number for the left margin, press **Enter**, enter the appropriate number for the right margin, and press **Enter**. Press **F7** to return to the document.

- Notice that the text has been formatted for the new line length. This has resulted in footnotes being moved from the bottom of the page. To move each footnote, move the cursor to the beginning of the footnote, press **Alt + F4**, highlight the footnote, press **Ctrl + F4**, **1** for block, **1** for move, move the cursor to where the footnote should appear, and press **Enter**. Footnotes assume the default one-inch left and right margins.

- If using the footnote commands **Ctrl + F7** to create the footnote entries, you must change the margin settings at the footnote editing screen (**Ctrl-F7, 1, 2**). At that screen, use **Shift + F8**.

- You may have to move a footnote more than one time as you experiment with exactly where it should be placed.

Application 23: Letterhead Template

- Notice that the letterhead form developed in Application 19 will be used for this application. You may want to switch to the typeover mode as you enter the text.

- Extensive text editing features will be used to revise a memorandum created for one purpose to be suitable for sending to another person.

Application 24: Simulation

- No new functions are introduced in this application. Several functions will be combined. This application also involves incorporating data from an electronic spreadsheet, another productivity tool, into a business letter.

Application 25: Report Cover Page

- The major effectiveness of a cover page depends on whether or not the material on the page has a good appearance. Although you are provided considerable freedom to design the cover page, compare your cover page layout with the following dimensions: "MAIL ORDER BUYING" begins on line 18, "Prepared for" begins on line 32, and "by" begins on line 50.

Application 26: Table of Contents

- Change the margin format to agree with the dimensions required for the document—1.5-inch left margin, 1-inch right and bottom margins, and 1.5-inch top margin.

- The dot leaders are keyed by pressing **Alt-F6**, **Alt-F6** after you key the section name, for example, Introduction.

Application Note: WordPerfect includes a feature that will automatically generate a table of contents. However, it is used primarily for lengthy documents.

Application 27: Manuscript

- Change the margin format to use the report dimensions. See the tutorial for Application 26.

- Notice that the top margin will be 1.5 inches on the first page but only 1 inch on all other pages of the manuscript.

- To use pagination to number the pages automatically, position the cursor at the beginning of the text where page numbering will begin, press **Shift + F8, 2, 6, 4, 3** to select position of page number on the page, and press **F7** to return to the document. Notice that choosing *9* instead of *3* can be used to turn page numbering off. To suppress the page numbering to the bottom on page 1, press **Shift + F8, 2, 8, 3, Y, F7**.

- As the document prints, the page numbers will appear on the pages.

Application 28: Bibliography

- Prepare the bibliography entries using the hanging indention style, which indents all lines except the first for each entry.

- Set a tab setting for a 5-space indention. After keying the first line and pressing **Enter** to begin the second line, press **F4** to indent from the left margin up to the tab setting. Each line will wrap around and return to the indention. After completing the entire entry, press **Enter** and the indention will be exited with a return of the cursor to the left margin. Notice that entries should be in alphabetical order. This arrangement should be made prior to keying the bibliography.

Application 29: Legal Complaint

- This application involves typing a legal document. This type of document often uses a 10-space paragraph indention. Change your tab setting to permit this indention.

- Several good questions are raised in the Review section. You may want to look at these items prior to keying the document.

Application 30: Form Letter

- Form letters are documents in which most of the information does not change from one copy to another, but some of the information, such as names and addresses, may differ in each copy. The main letter is called the primary document. The variable information (names and addresses in this application) is stored in the secondary document.

- To create the primary document enter text up to the point where a variable is to be inserted and then press **Shift + F9** and **1** to choose field. Enter **1** to select the first field of the record for this location and press **Enter**. Repeat this process for the next location where text will be inserted, except enter **2** to select the second field. Save the document.

- To create the secondary document enter the first record (through the ZIP code in this application) and press **F9** to end the field. Enter the second record (through the person's last name in this application) and press **F9** to end the field. Since this is the end of the record, press **Shift + F9** and **2** or **E** to end the record. Repeat this procedure for each of the remaining three records. Save the document.

- Press **F7** and respond as needed to clear the screen prior to the merging process.

- To produce copies of the form letter, press **Ctrl + F9** and **1** or **M** to choose merge. Enter the name of the file containing the saved letter as the primary file. Enter the name of the file containing the saved variables as the secondary file. You should see * *Merging* * on the screen to indicate that merging is taking place.

- The merged form letters should appear on your screen. You can now save and/or print the documents.

- Mail merge is a very specific procedure. If any of the coding is in error, the procedure will not take place. If the error is not apparent, you may find it easier to begin at the first step and code again.

Application 31: Legal Complaint Template

- Use the legal complaint completed in Application 29 for this application.

- Use the search and replace option to change the text. To change *Memphis* to *Germantown* follow these steps: Press **Alt + F2** and enter **N** so you do not have to confirm each replacement throughout the document. Enter **Memphis** at the *Srch:* prompt and press **F2**. Enter **Germantown** at the *Replace with:* prompt and press **F2**. The search and replace procedure should now be completed in your document.

Application 32: Form Letter

- This application expands on the mail/merge feature presented in Application 30.

- Notice that there will be four variable insertions in the letter. Follow the steps presented, but remember that the merges will be numbered 1, 2, 3, and 4 in the primary file. Save the primary document.

- Remember to press **F9** to insert an end-of-field code after each of the four fields in each record and to press **Shift + F9** and **2** or **E** to end each of the four records. Save the secondary document.

- Merge and print the form letters.

Application 33: Customized Letter

- Text that you can use repeatedly in a variety of files is called boilerplating. Enter the text for each of the seven paragraphs and save each one individually with the first paragraph being P1, the second P2, and so forth.

- Enter the text up to the point where a paragraph is needed, press **Shift + F10** and the drive and file name such as **A:P1**, and press **Enter**. The paragraph appears on the screen quickly. Repeat this process until the document is completed. Then save (if desired) and print the document.

- Repeat this process for each of the four letters.

Application 34: Legal Complaint Template

- Retrieve the legal complaint document completed in Application 29 and convert it to a form document.

- Delete the text and insert the merge variable code at each of the 10 points indicated on the document. Save the primary document.

- Prepare the secondary file. Note that there are 10 fields and 3 records.

- Notice that some fields are repeated in the secondary file. A field can be used more than one time in the primary document. Therefore, you have an option of creating only seven fields. However, be careful to match the field numbers in the primary document with the order in the secondary document.

Application 35: Letter Template

- Boilerplating will be used to create three additional letters in this application. Since the paragraphs were already stored in Application 33, the only procedures needed relate to retrieving the stored paragraphs and keying the text portion of each of the three letters. This is a very common application in a word processing office.

Application 36: Form Letter Template

- Use the primary document created in Application 30 for this application. The document should already be coded, so you will only have to retrieve the secondary file created in Application 30, delete the record for Betty J. Maniel, and add and code the two additional records.

- Maintenance of mailing lists takes much time in many offices. This application illustrates this procedure.

Application 37: Manuscript Template

- Use the manuscript created in Application 27 for this application.

- Make the indicated text editing changes. Move footnotes, if needed, to assure that they appear at the bottom of the page where the text citation appears. Additional practice with the search and replace feature is provided.

Application 38: Simulation

- This application involves putting all the parts of the manuscript together into one document. Make the text editing changes, move footnotes, and so forth as requested on the assignment sheet. You will use several features introduced in previous applications.

Application 39: Budget

- Format the tab setting to permit a tab for the second column.

- There are six basic steps for using the math feature: setting the tabs, defining the math columns, turning on math, typing the table, performing the calculations, and turning off math.

- Set left and right margins as needed.

- Set tabs in the usual way, using right tabs for the amounts.

- Press **Alt + F7, 3, 3,** use the down arrow key to move down to *Number of Digits to Right,* and press **0, F7,** and **1** to define the math column and turn on the math function.

- Key the table.

- On the last line where the total will appear, tab to the location where the total will appear and enter **+**.

- To calculate the total, press **Alt + F7, 3,** and **4** to calculate. The total appears to the left of the + symbol.

Application 40: Trial Balance

- This application involves an extension of the math procedures presented in Application 39. You will add two columns of figures in this application.

Application 41: Organization Chart

- Use line draw to make the organization chart. Review the procedures for line draw by recalling the tutorial for Application 7. Although this application presents a much more complex use of line draw, the basic procedures introduced in Application 7 should be sufficient here.

- Remember to do the text portion first. Then use the line draw feature to draw all of the lines. Then erase lines, as appropriate.

Application 42: Flyer

- Enter the text for the flyer.

- For the graphics, use the clip art files available with WordPerfect. To import the clip art files, place the cursor at the point where the graphic will appear, press **Alt + F9**, **1** for figure, **1** to create, **1** for filename prompt, **CALENDAR.WPG**, and **Enter** to return to the *Definition: Figure menu*. (Notice that you can change the size and other definitions at this time, if desired.) Press **F7** to return to the document. The figure should now be in your document. Press **Shift + F7** and **6** to view the document with the graphic.

- Continue this procedure for the other graphic. The filename is CLOCK.WPG.

- Save and print the document. Notice that your printer may take longer to print the document because it contains graphics.

Application 43: Table

- Key the letter up to the point where the spreadsheet table is to be imported.

- Press **Ctrl + F5** and **1** for DOS text. Press **2** to retrieve. Enter **P-EXER43.PRN** and press **Enter**. The spreadsheet should now be on your screen below your cursor. (The *A*: indicates that the spreadsheet file is in drive A. If not, enter the appropriate drive designation.)

- Continue to key the remainder of the letter. Then save and print the document.

Application 44: Budget Template

- Use the budget completed in Application 39 during this application. You should be in the typeover mode as changes are made to the figures in the budget. Notice that the total does not change as you revise figures.

- After the figures have been changed, press **Alt + F7** and **3** to choose math. Press **4** to calculate. The new total should now be computed.

Application 45: Organization Chart

- Use line draw to add positions to the organization chart partially completed in Application 41.

Application 46: Simulation

- This simulation involves several features that were introduced in previous applications.

WordPerfect
Command Card

Backspace	Backspace Key
Base Font	Ctrl + F8,4
Binding	Shift + F7,B
Block	Alt + F4
Block Move/Copy (Block on)	Ctrl + F4
Bold	F6
Bottom Margin	Shift + F8,2
Cancel	F1
Cancel Hyphenation	F1
Cancel Print Job(s)	Shift + F7,4,1
Case Conversion (Block on)	Shift + F3
Center	Shift + F6
Center Page Top to Bottom	Shift + F8,2
Coded Space	Home, Space bar
Column, Move/Copy (Block on)	Ctrl + F4
Columns, Text	Alt + F7
Conditional End of Page	Shift + F8
Copy (List Files)	F5,Enter,8
Date/Outline	Shift + F5
Decimal/Align Character	Shift + F8,4
Delete	Del Key
Delete to End of Line (EOL)	Ctrl + End
Delete to End of Page (EOP)	Ctrl + Pg Dn
Delete (List Files)	F5,Enter,2
Delete Word	Ctrl + Backspace
Delete Word (cursor to beginning)	Home, Backspace
Delete Word (cursor to end)	Home, Del
Display All Print Jobs	Shift + F7,4,3
Display Pitch	Shift + F8,3
Endnote	Ctrl + F7
Escape	Esc Key
Exit	F7
Flush Right	Alt + F6
Force Odd/Even Page	Shift + F8,2
Font	Ctrl + F8
Footnote	Ctrl + F7
Format: Document menu	Shift + F8,3
Format: Line menu	Shift + F8,1
Format: Other menu	Shift + F8,4
Format: Page menu	Shift + F8,2
Full Document (Print)	Shift + F7,1
Go (Start Printing)	Shift + F7,4,4
Graphics	Alt + F9
Hard Page	Ctrl + Enter
Hard Return	Enter
Headers or Footers	Shift + F8,2
Help	F3
Hyphenation On/Off	Shift + F8,1
Hyphenation Zone	Shift + F8,1
->Indent	F4
->Indent<-	Shift + F4
Index	Alt + F5
Initial Codes/Font	Shift + F8,3
Justification On/Off	Shift + F8,1
Line Draw	Ctrl + F3,2
Line Height	Shift + F8,1
Line Numbering	Shift + F8,1
Line Spacing	Shift + F8,1
List (Block on)	Alt + F5
List Files	F5,Enter
Look	F5,Enter,6
Macro	Alt + F10
Macro Def	Ctrl + F10
Margin Release	Shift + Tab
Margins	Shift + F8,1
Mark Text	Alt + F5
Math	Alt + F7
Merge	Ctrl + F9
Merge Codes	Shift + F9
Merge R	F9
Move . . . . :	Ctrl + F4
Name Search	F5,Enter,N
New Page Number	Shift + F8,2
Number of Copies	Shift + F7,N
Other Directory	F5,Enter,7
Overstrike	Shift + F8,4
Page Numbering	Shift + F8,2
Page (Print)	Shift + F7,2
Paper Size/Type	Shift + F8,2
Print Block (Block on)	Shift + F7
Print: Control Printer menu . . .	Shift + F7,4
Print a Document	Shift + F7,3
Print (List Files)	F5,Enter,4
Print menu	Shift + F7
Redline	Ctrl + F8,2,8
Rename (List Files)	F5,Enter,3
Replace	Alt + F2
Retrieve	Shift + F10
Retrieve (List Files)	F5,Enter
Reveal Codes	Alt + F3
Rush Print Job	Shift + F7,4,2
Save	F10
Screen	Ctrl + F3
Search (Backward)	Shift + F2
Search (Forward)	F2
Select Printer	Shift + F7,S
Setup	Shift + F1
Shell	Ctrl + F1
Sort	Ctrl + F9
Spacing	Shift + F8,1
Spell	Ctrl + F2
Stop Printing	Shift + F7,4,5
Strikeout (Block on)	Ctrl + F8,2,9
Style	Alt + F8
Super/Subscript	Ctrl + F8,1
Suppress	Shift + F8,2
Switch	Shift + i3
Tab Align	Ctrl + F6
Tab Set	Shift + F8,1
Table of Authorities (block on)	Alt + F5
Table of Contents (block on)	Alt + F5
Text In/Out	Ctrl + F5
Thesaurus	Alt + F1
Top Margin	Shift + F8,2
Typeover	Ins Key
Type-thru	Shift + F7,5
Undelete	F1
Underline	F8
Underline Style	Shift + F8,4
Widow/Orphan	Shift + F8,1
Word Count	Ctrl + F2
Word Search	F5,Enter,9

CURSOR MOVEMENT COMMANDS

Word Left	Ctrl + Left Arrow
Word Right	Ctrl + Right Arrow
End of Line	End
Screen Left	Home, Left Arrow
Screen Right	Home, Right Arrow
Screen Down	Home, Down Arrow
Screen Up	Home, Up Arrow
Page Down	Dn Key
Page Up	Pg Up Key
Specific Page	Ctrl + Home, #, Enter
Beginning of Text	Home, Home, Up Arrow
End of Text	Home, Home, Down Arrow

Microsoft Word
Command Card

Annotation	Esc,F,A
Bold	Alt+B
Bookmark	Esc,F,K
Cancel command	Esc
Center	Alt+C
Change case	Control+F4
Columns	Esc,F,D,L
Copy	Alt+F3 or Esc,C
Delete document	Esc,T,D or Esc,L,D,D
Delete text	Shift+Del
Delete text to scrap	Del
Division break	Control+Enter
Double spacing	Alt+2
Double underline	Alt+D
Font change	Alt+F8 or Esc,F,C
Footnote	Esc,F,F
Glossary, create	Esc,C
Glossary, insert	F3
Glossary, load	Esc,T,G,L
Glossary, print	Esc,P,G
Glossary, save	Esc,T,G,S
Hanging indent	Alt+T
Hidden text	Alt+E
Hyphen, automatic	Esc,L,H
Hyphen, nonbreaking	Control+Shift+hyphen
Hyphen, optional	Control+hyphen
Indent, decrease left	Alt+M
Indent, first line	Alt+F
Indent, increase left and right	Alt+Q
Indent, left	Alt+N
Index	Esc,L,I
Italics	Alt+I
Jump, annotation	Esc,J,A
Jump, footnote	Esc,J,F
Jump, specific page	Alt+F5 or Esc,J,P
Justify paragraph	Alt+J
Line draw	Control+F5
Line spacing	Esc,F,P
Load document	Control+F7 or Esc,T,L
Macro, edit	Esc,I
Macro, cancel	Esc
Macro, record	Shift+F3
Macro, run	F3 or Control+assigned key
Margins	Esc,F,D,M
Math, calculate	F2
Merge	Esc,T,M
Merge to document	Esc,P,M,D
Merge to printer	Esc,P,M,P
New line command	Shift+Enter
Nonbreaking space	Control+spacebar
Overtype	F5
Page break	Control+Shift+Enter
Page numbers	Esc,F,D,P
Paragraph, align left	Alt+L
Paragraph, align right	Alt+R
Print preview	Control+F9 or Esc,P,V
Print, document	Control+F8 or Esc,P,P
Print, hidden text	Esc,P,O
Print, line numbers	Esc,F,D,N
Print, stop	Esc
Quit Word	Esc,Q
Repaginate	Esc,P,R
Revision marks, add	Esc,F,M,O
Revision marks, remove	Esc,F,M,R
Ruler display	Esc,O
Running heads, footer	Alt+F2 or Esc,F,R
Running heads, header	Control+F2 or Esc,F,R
Save	Control+F10 or Esc,T,S

Screen borders display	Esc,O
Search, character format	Esc,F,E,C
Search, paragraph format	Esc,F,E,P
Search, text	Esc,S
Show layout	Alt+F4 or Esc,O
Small caps	Alt+K
Sort	Esc,L,A
Spell	Alt+F6 or Esc,L,S
Strikethrough	Alt+S
Styles, apply	Alt+key code
Styles, attach style sheet	Esc,F,S,A
Styles, copy	Esc,G,C
Styles, create style sheet	Esc,G,T,S
Styles, create by example	Alt+F10 or Esc,F,S,R
Styles, create with Gallery	Esc,G,I
Styles, delete	Esc,G,D
Styles, print style sheet	Esc,G,P
Styles, view style sheet	Esc,G
Subscript	Alt+hyphen
Superscript	Alt+equal sign
Table of contents	Esc,L,T
Tabs, clear all tab stops	Esc,F,T,R
Tabs, insert or delete	Alt+F1 or Esc,F,T,S
Thesaurus	Control+F6 or Esc,L,E
Underline	Alt+U
Undo editing changes	Shift+F1 or Esc,U
Uppercase format	Esc,F,C
Windows, activate next window	F1
Windows, clear	Esc,T,C,W
Windows, close	Esc,W,C
Windows, open	Esc,W,S
Windows, zoom	Control+F1

Highlight Movement

Line above	Up arrow
Line below	Down arrow
Character left	Left arrow
Character right	Right arrow
Beginning of line	Home
End of line	End
Previous column	Control+5(keypad)+left arrow
Next column	Control+5(keypad)+right arrow
Top of window	Control+Home
Bottom of window	Control+End
Beginning of document	Control+PgUp
End of document	Control+PgDn
Previous word	Control+left arrow
Next word	Control+right arrow
Previous paragraph	Control+up arrow
Next paragraph	Control+down arrow
Scroll up window	PgUp
Scroll down window	PgDn

Selecting Text

Previous word	F7
Next word	F8
Previous sentence	Shift+F7
Next sentence	Shift+F8
Previous paragraph	F9
Next paragraph	F10
Current line	Shift+F9
Whole document	Shift+F10
Extend (on/off)	F6
Column (on/off)	Shift+F6